The STOIC RIDER

The STOIC RIDER

Philosophy in Motion

LOUISA SWADEN

THROTTLE
& THOUGHT
PRESS

The Stoic Rider
© 2025 Louisa Swaden
Published by Throttle & Thought Press

All rights reserved. No part of this publication may be reproduced, stored in a retrieval system, or transmitted in any form or by any means – electronic, mechanical, photocopying, recording, or otherwise – without prior written permission of the publisher, except for brief quotations used in reviews, critical articles, or educational purposes.

For permissions or rights enquiries, contact:
info@existentialbiker.com

Throttle & Thought Press
www.existentialbiker.com

ISBN (Paperback): 978-1-0682107-0-9
ISBN (eBook): 978-1-0682107-1-6

Cover design by Alicia Paulson
Interior design by Alicia Paulson
Cover photo by Aruthan Muhunthan

This is a work of nonfiction. Some names and identifying details have been changed to protect privacy.

The moral right of the author has been asserted.

Printed in the United Kingdom
First Edition

For Teddy, Avery, and Willow.
Remember, you can be and do anything.
"Do what you love and the rest will follow."
— *The Existential Nana*

And to Daf, who reminds us that there are many ways to experience and express love in this world.

"The trouble is, you think you have time."

— Buddha

Table of Contents

Introduction 1

PART ONE: RESILIENCE 11

Chapter 1: The Obstacle Is the Way 13
Chapter 2: Choose Your Line 35
Chapter 3: *Amor Fati* – Love of Fate 49

PART TWO: INTENTION 61

Chapter 4: Memento Mori – Remember You Must Die 63
Chapter 5: Stillness in Motion 83
Chapter 6: Riding with the World 103

PART THREE: DIRECTION 119

Chapter 7: Where You Look Is Where You Go 121
Chapter 8: No One Rides Alone 139
Chapter 9: Ride With Virtue 159

PART FOUR: EXPANSION 179

Chapter 10: Check Your Mirrors 181
Chapter 11: Answer the Call 201
Chapter 12: The Road Is the Teacher 215

Epilogue	221
Acknowledgments	227
Endnotes	231
References	235
About the Author	245
Keep Riding. Keep Reflecting.	247

Introduction

The Road Ahead

"It is not death that a man should fear, but he should fear never beginning to live."
— Marcus Aurelius

I WAS ALL AT ONCE five, ten, thirty, fifty years old — every age I'd ever lived, suddenly present, layered and vivid. Each scraped knee, each burst of uncontainable laughter. Failed attempts, late-night conversations that mattered, loving kisses, heartbeats, half-forgotten smiles of those I've loved and lost — now lit me from within.

The world around me faded, yet my awareness had never felt sharper. Nothing else existed. No need to analyse, to perform, to explain. Just a quiet, steady sense of being — undiluted, unfiltered, *enough*.

139 mph!

It was pure, existential bliss.

And that's what bliss really is when you take away the marketing – just the absolute clarity of not wanting to be anywhere else.

No words will ever quite reach it. Language, for all its cleverness, tends to trip over its own shoelaces when it tries to describe these moments. But maybe that's the point. Maybe these moments exist *outside* the frame. They aren't there to be captured. Only lived.

But how did I get here?

I'd only met the bike twenty-four hours earlier. A snow-white Hayabusa bought hastily in Salt Lake City. It was still a stranger to me, and yet somehow, in the hundred-mile stretch back through the Utah desert, we'd found each other. Not with spectacle but with quiet inevitability. I didn't tame it. We simply came into step.

By the time I reached the flats, it didn't feel like a new bike anymore. It felt like fate. The kind of fate you don't discover until you've stopped resisting the journey and started listening to it.

I'd come a long way from the UK for this – logistically, yes, but also emotionally. This wasn't some performative stunt or a tidy box ticked off a bucket list.

This wasn't about records. Or speed. Or glory. This was about something far deeper: the moment I stopped running from fear and chose to ride alongside it.

I was there to say, *I'm alive*. And *this* – this full-body presence, this hum of courage – is what that feels like.

The Bonneville Salt Flats, for the uninitiated, look like somewhere between the moon and an overexposed dream. Thirty thousand acres of shimmering white silence. The skeletal remains of an ancient lake, dried out over millennia and left behind like a secret. In the early 20th century, someone clever realised it was perfect for speed trials, and the legend of Bonneville was born. Since then, the area has become synonymous with records and extreme speeds, hosting legendary events like Speed Week, where drivers push their vehicles to the limit.

All the life-changing moments, the pain, the doubt, the chance meetings, all the people I'd met, all the twists and turns of my recent life – had somehow conspired to place me right there, at that starting line. It was a certainty I felt in my very core. On the salt. Gloved hands. Full leathers. A bike I'd only met twenty-four hours earlier.

I would not let anything get in my way that day – so woe betide anything that tried to stop me!

Eighteen months earlier, I was afraid to go over fifty miles per hour.

Not metaphorically. Literally. A twist of the throttle and my stomach would lurch. My brain would shout, *What the hell are you doing?* I wasn't born a rider. I didn't come to it young and wild. I learned at seventeen for practical reasons – just as a way to get to work. I passed my full test at twenty-four, then didn't touch a bike again for over two decades.

But life, with its impeccable sense of timing, brought me back. At first tentatively. Then with increasing hunger. And eventually, with total surrender.

I recall the moment the The Existential Biker was born. I remember the name coming to me in a dream. But when she became real? That was Bonneville.

The wait at the start line was both a moment and a lifetime. The horizon buzzed. The radio hissed. I knew – as sure as I was breathing – that I was at peace with my fate, and I accepted it. There were no words left, just the senses. The sun, the salt, the horizon all thundered through my veins. And then – nothing. The kind of silence that isn't empty, but full. Not the absence of noise, but the absence of resistance. No inner chatter. No fear disguised as logic. Just presence.

I wasn't there to cheat death. I was there to acknowledge it.

And in that quiet agreement – me on the bike, death on the salt – we nodded to one another. No rush. No retreat.

This run didn't start at the salt – it started with a friend whose flame lit the way. Just before the run, he'd told me about the fire I needed to feel – that sense of unshakeable purpose, total commitment, and all-consuming focus on what lay ahead across those wet salt crystals. I'd heard his words at the time, but I didn't fully grasp their weight until now.

He called it *the flame* – that force inside him that burned through fear and doubt, turning them into raw energy and unstoppable momentum. He'd passed it to me, and in that instant, I felt it – a flicker deep in my gut, sparking to life. A fire that would consume the moment, reduce it to pure energy and action, and incinerate fear, doubt, and any idea of failure.

And then the flame rose. Small. Steady. Certain.

It said: *RIDE.*

That's what Bonneville gave me. Not identity. Not adrenaline. But clarity.

The kind that only arrives when you surrender the illusion of control and choose to move forward anyway.

This book was born in that moment.

This isn't a manual for riders. It's not a book of philosophy lectures either. You don't need to be a motorcyclist. You don't need to know Epictetus from Elvis. You need to have known fear – and wondered how to keep moving anyway.

Because life unfolds the same way the road does. Not in theory. Not in epiphanies. But mile by mile. Sometimes in beauty. Sometimes in chaos.

And now and then, if you're paying attention, it offers a flash of clarity that rearranges everything.

I realise now how that moment changed me and what it taught me. Not to be fearless. Not to chase danger. But to live with eyes open, hands steady, and heart anchored in the present.

That's the real teaching.

At its core, Stoicism asks one disarmingly simple question: *What's in your control?*

Your answer to that question shapes your life more than almost anything else.

It shaped mine.

Out on the salt flats, I understood the risks. I'd done the sums. Heard the warnings. "That bike's too powerful." "You're not ready." "The salt's unpredictable." Fair points, all of them. But I'd already made peace with the only bit that mattered: my mindset, my presence, my willingness to meet the moment as it was – not as I wished it to be.

It wasn't recklessness. It was presence. The conscious choice to stop deferring life. To stop waiting for someone to tap me on the shoulder and say, *You're allowed now*.

I'd waited long enough.

That's what this book is really about.

Not about riding motorcycles, it's about learning how to ride through life itself. With a bit more grace. A touch more grit. And a fair helping of curiosity. With enough awareness to know when to push, and enough trust to know when to let go.

It's about building a quiet kind of resilience – the kind that doesn't shout. Just an honest reckoning with who you are, what you value, and how you show up when life starts to wobble.

* * *

The journey unfolds in four parts, each a pillar of the R.I.D.E. roadmap:

PART ONE – **R**ESILIENCE
How we meet obstacles and make sense of setbacks.

PART TWO – **I**NTENTION
How to live with presence and purpose.

PART THREE – **D**IRECTION
Where we choose to go and how we stay aligned.

PART FOUR – **E**XPANSION
The lifelong practice of growth, reflection, and becoming.

This is a book for those who want to lean into life's curves rather than brace against them. To trade survival for steady, joyful momentum. To ride, not just roam.

We begin with resilience – how we meet obstacles and make sense of setbacks. Then we'll talk about intention – how to live with presence and purpose. From there, we explore direction – where we choose to go and how we stay aligned. And finally, expansion – how to cultivate the lifelong practice of growth, reflection, and becoming.

This isn't about being perfect. Just progress. Not becoming someone else. Just becoming more fully *yourself*.

You might be wondering – why motorcycles? Why not just write a book about Stoicism?

Because a bike strips things down. There's nowhere to hide.

Every corner teaches you something about fear, control, or trust. Every mile demands attention. Every ride is a lesson in impermanence. In humility. In focus. In joy.

There's something about that combination – the vulnerability and the freedom – that makes it the perfect companion to Stoic thought.

You don't need to love bikes to understand that. You just need to have lived long enough to know that life isn't simple. That it hurts sometimes. That beauty arrives in odd places. And that you want something solid to hold when things fall apart.

That's what Stoicism offers. Not tricks. Not perfect answers. Just a way to stay upright when the wind picks up.

The road ahead isn't straight. It isn't smooth. But it is *yours*.

PART ONE

RESILIENCE

The road has potholes. The engine stalls. Plans unravel. You're out in the world with just your breath, your balance, and the choice to keep moving.

Resilience shows up in the way you adjust your grip or slow your pace without losing direction. These chapters sit in the moments that test you — not dramatic, just real. A sharp turn. A stretch of silence. A rough patch handled with calm. You move through, not around.

Chapter 1

The Obstacle Is the Way

*"The impediment to action advances action.
What stands in the way becomes the way."*
— Marcus Aurelius

D REAMS DON'T BREAK QUIETLY. They snap like a valve stem on the salt flats – sudden, cheap, and final.

That day – *the* day – wasn't smooth. It rarely is, when things matter. We were within touching distance. The sun was already creeping high over Bonneville, the salt glowing like a film set that someone had forgotten to sweep.

The Hayabusa had passed almost every part of the tech inspection. Powertrain – check. Leathers – check. Kill switch, safety wiring, fire extinguisher – check, check, check.

But then, a pause. The inspector's glove tapped the wheel like a judge's gavel. His frown said what the rulebook did: You don't belong here.

"Valve stems," the inspector said. "They're rubber. They need to be metal."

I blinked. Surely not *this*? Not some fiddly little bit of kit no one had mentioned?

A five-dollar part. That's what stood between us and Bonneville. Not the engine. Not the years of prep. A rubber-wheel valve stem the rulebook insisted must be metal.

It's a strange thing, the moment your expectations crash. The mind rushes in with its usual solutions: anger, blame, despair. The voice in your head starts muttering that old story – *You're not meant for this. You don't belong here.*

But Stoicism isn't a philosophy for when things go to plan. It's for exactly this.

As Epictetus reminds us, "It's not what happens to you, but how you react to it that matters."

And I had a choice. Stand there sulking under the Utah sun, or move.

So we moved. Fast.

We didn't panic – but we didn't waste time either. We rolled the bike straight back onto the trailer and hit the road. Wendover wasn't far, but with the pressure mounting, every minute felt loaded. Thirty minutes later, we pulled up to S&R Auto on Wendover Boulevard. It was packed. The owner was buried in jobs and said we'd need to wait a couple of hours. I begged. I pleaded. I explained everything – how far we'd come, how tight our window was. He listened, but the answer was the same. The fire chief's truck was ahead of us, and he wasn't budging.

We waited. Forty minutes passed. No sign of progress. We kicked around bolts on the floor and stared down mechanics who wouldn't meet our eyes. The bike just sat there, static and helpless. Then Suzanne heard that the rookie course was closing early – rough salt, a safety risk. One hour left. We weren't going to make it back in time.

That should have been the end.

But it wasn't.

Eleanora showed up out of nowhere with homemade class and number designation stickers she'd made with a keen artistic eye and a Sharpie. It was a tiny win, but a reminder we weren't totally alone. Then Vito stepped in – literally got on the floor and helped the mechanic change out the stems. If he hadn't, we'd have lost another hour easily. He got us out of there. He saved the day – and not for the first time. He and Suzanne had been with me every step of the way, believing in me more than I did in myself.

Back at tech, a tense, quick final inspection, and yes! – the Hayabusa had passed. Stickers slapped on. Numbers applied. Tape on the fairings. It looked like a real race bike now, ready for the flats. But the clock said otherwise. The rookie course was definitely shut. We missed it.

I still went to ask.

I found an inspector and poured it all out. The fire chief. The scramble. The dream. I didn't hold back. I was emotional, probably rambling. He listened, then said six words I'll never forget:

"Oh yeah, you can do it."

Not on the rookie course, but on the long course. That was better. That was everything.

It was happening.

I found Jim Hoogerhyde, one of SCTA's senior course inspectors. He told me what I needed to hear. He gave me not just safety tips but real confidence. He explained how the salt would hold me, and how centrifugal force would do its job.

Let me explain the effect Jim had on me. The previous twenty-four hours had been among the most intense of my life. I was running on adrenaline, anxiety, and barely any sleep. The heat inside my leathers and fireproof underlayer was suffocating – I could feel the sweat pooling behind my knees, my hands shaking despite the desert wind. And underneath all of it was something harder to admit: I just wanted someone to hold my hand. I missed my family. I missed the comfort of a hug, the simple grounding of someone saying, *"You've got this. I'm here. I'm watching."* I needed someone who understood what this meant – not just the speed, but the courage it had taken to even get here. His calm tone and sun-weathered smile gave me exactly what I needed in that moment. He had that steady presence – the kind my dad once gave me, before life cut that time short. It was as close to a hug as I was going to get. And somehow, it was enough.

I asked him, nervously, "What if I go over the rookie limit of 149 mph?" He smiled and said, "Don't."

But he also gave me a target. If I could get over 125 mph, I'd earn my D license. One shot. That's all I'd get today.

It was late in the day and the salt was slushy, like snow driven over hundreds of times. It had been raining hard in the lead-up to Speed Week, and conditions were rough – potentially unrideable as safety was of paramount concern. This was already day six of seven and only the third day they'd allowed any racing. The shadows were long. But I was ready.

The rest happened fast. Leathers on. Helmet down. A quick nod and word of advice about choosing the best line from the starter. No countdown. No lights. Just a look and a go.

I don't remember every second of the run. Just the feeling: calm, focused, totally alive. I kept the throttle balanced. Guessed the speed, knowing the dial lied because of the slippage from the back wheel on the salt.

Passed the light markers. Slowed down carefully – no brakes, no sudden deceleration, just a smooth, almost spiritual mile of absolute stillness. That far out there was no one. No crowds, no cameras, nothing. Just blue sky and white salt for miles upon miles. Pulled off the course. Stopped at the designated pick-up point.

Then I waited.

Jim came over first. He was grinning as he handed me the small piece of paper that looked more like an ordinary printed fuel receipt. On top, in thick black pen, were the scrawled the words: "Perfect" and "D". I couldn't read them; I couldn't focus. So he told me.

"139 mph."

Rookie pass. D license. First time. Only chance.

Moments later, I found out they'd shut the final course. Speed Week had closed a day early.

Walking with the Stoics, Riding with Life

There's a certain moment when the engine's running fine, the sky is clear, and yet something inside you hums with restlessness. It's not about the ride anymore. It's about the rider. You stop asking, *Why is this happening to me?* and instead begin to wonder, *What is this asking of me?* That change in question isn't semantics – it's direction. It doesn't move outward, toward blame or explanation. It turns inward, toward awareness.

Modern psychology has a name for this – *cognitive reappraisal* – which is a rather clinical phrase for something remarkably human. It's the same engine running beneath Stoic thought: You can't control the terrain, but you can change how you ride across it. And how you ride shapes everything. Resist every bump and corner and you'll be exhausted before lunch. But adjust your grip, shift your weight a little, and suddenly the road starts to speak. You move with it, not against it. The bumps don't vanish. But they stop defining the ride.

I used to think clarity came from certainty. If I could plan it all and map every step, I'd stay safe. But that's not how the road works. I tried to outrun discomfort, silence doubt with spreadsheets and strategies. None of it stuck. What stuck was the moment I stopped resisting. Not collapsing. Just pausing. Listening. Long enough to ask:

What is this teaching me I wouldn't have chosen to learn?
Who am I becoming because of this, not despite it?
Is there a way to meet this with less friction?

The Stoics weren't selling a shortcut. They offered a compass. Not to avoid storms, but to help you steer through them with your hands on the controls and your eyes open. Not hardened. Just present.

Stoicism isn't suppression. That's the common misunderstanding. It's not about ignoring your emotions – it's about respecting them enough to pause. To sort them. To know which ones are visitors and which ones are guides. Epictetus said that we don't control events, only our responses. But that's not passivity. It's precision. Attention. Saying, *This is the situation – so how will I stand inside it?*

Marcus Aurelius once wrote to himself, not as a ruler, but as a man trying to stay upright, "You have power over your mind – not outside events. Realise this, and you will find strength."[1] That strength isn't bravado. It's alignment. The engine humming just right. The self tuned in – not to noise, but to signal.

We live in a culture obsessed with outcomes. The Stoics weren't. They were obsessed with effort. With choice. With how you ride your ride when the wind picks up.

The Road Is the Teacher

There's a particular silence that only happens on a bike. Not the silence of absence, but of focus. The engine hums beneath you – a kind of mechanical heartbeat – and everything else, for a moment, falls respectfully quiet. The emails wait. The dishes wait. Even your own internal monologue, usually full of unsolicited advice, takes a back seat.

You're not defeating the road. You're riding with it.

Every curve is a question. Every gust of wind, a raised eyebrow.

Every patch of gravel, a polite warning that you are not, in fact, in charge of everything.

An experienced rider knows this. They don't attack the road. They adjust. Weight shifts. Hands loosen. Breathing slows. They aren't predicting. They're participating. And participation, as it turns out, is a far more reliable form of control than brute force.

This isn't giving up. It's tuning in.

The Stoics, of course, understood this. They just didn't call it counter-steering.

Epictetus said, "We cannot choose our external circumstances, but we can always choose how we respond to them."[2] Which sounds terribly noble until you're doing 50 mph in the rain with a lorry spraying you like a hosepipe test. Then it becomes less of an idea and more of a practice.

Seneca once advised, "A setback has often cleared the way for greater prosperity. Many things have fallen only to rise to more exalted heights."[3] Quite right. But he never had to pick up a dropped Triumph in a layby outside Cheltenham.

Still, he had a point. We learn more from the unplanned detour than the mapped route.

Riding teaches humility quickly. The bike does not care about your ego. If you approach a corner too proud, too stiff, or too certain, the road corrects you without ceremony. But meet it with curiosity – with the quiet competence that comes from attention – and it responds.

This is the soul of Stoicism. Not cold detachment, but warm responsibility. You're not separate from the world. You're in it. With it. And your only real task is how well you attend to that fact.

Riders speak of flow states. The psychologists have other names for it, but the Stoics were there long before the TED Talks. "Concentrate every minute," Marcus Aurelius wrote, "on doing what's in front of you with precise and genuine seriousness, tenderly, willingly, with justice."[4] He may have been addressing imperial affairs, but the advice applies just as well to roundabouts in the rain.

And what if we lived more like this?

What if we stopped trying to control the journey, and paid better attention to how we move through it? What if we replaced resistance with curiosity, tightness with trust, bravado with presence?

The road is not your enemy. It is your teacher. And like the best teachers, it repeats the lesson patiently, again and again:

Loosen up. Pay attention. Try again.

Adversity and the Slightly Leaky Roof of the Soul

There comes a moment – not a grand, cinematic one, but the sort that slips in unnoticed between your morning coffee going cold and the fourth email marked "urgent" – when you begin to suspect your inner narrator might not be entirely reliable. The voice that mutters, *Why me?* or *It's always like this,* starts to sound more like a petulant teenager than the voice of reason.

The Stoics would have smiled at this. Not smugly, but knowingly. Epictetus reminded his students that it's not things themselves that trouble us, but our opinions about them.[5] In other words, the world isn't out to get you – it's just being the world. Your mind, on the other hand, is doing interpretive dance in a thunderstorm.

Some years ago, I found myself in just such a storm. A rather literal one. I was on one of my first trips abroad, riding an Indian Scout (I was only later to realise how coincidental my first choice of "real" bike was, when I watched *The World's Fastest Indian*), and after a month that felt like I'd been personally audited by fate – relationship gone sideways, work dribbling meaninglessly on, and a sleep pattern best described as 'aspirational.' Somewhere near Baden Baden, the heavens opened with theatrical flair. I pulled off the road, soaked, irritated, muttering something unrepeatable to no one in particular. Sure – I had wet gear on, but rain still persisted in running down my neck and into the hole I'd made through it so that my heated jacket could be wired into the battery. The jacket that was to later leave burn marks on my neck.

Then – because there's always a "then" in these stories – I just stood there.

No resolution. No sudden joy. Just a shift – small, but steady. I became aware of the rain not as punishment, but as presence. The steady hiss of it on the road, the drumming on my helmet, the gentle patter on leaves – each sound sharp and distinct, like the world had turned up its volume. The scent of wet earth and tarmac rose around me – raw, green, grounding. The storm hadn't singled me out. It wasn't cruel or personal. It simply *was*. Cold, relentless, necessary. Nature doing what nature does – without apology, without malice, without concern for my plans. And in that moment, I let it be. I let *me* be. Drenched, shivering, fully alive.

That's when I understood. The storm was never the problem. The problem was believing it shouldn't rain.

That's what the Stoics called *prosochē* – attention. Not mystical enlightenment, just the practice of noticing. Noticing that while you can't stop the rain, you can stop arguing with it. You can choose your posture in the downpour.

Modern psychology, of course, has its own terms. Cognitive behavioural therapy talks of reframing. Viktor Frankl called it meaning-making.[6] But the Stoics got there first – with a pen, a scroll, and the occasional toga.

Marcus Aurelius, who managed to run an empire and keep a journal (a fact that shames most of us), wrote: "If you are pained by external things, it is not they that disturb you, but your own judgment of them. And it is in your power to wipe out that judgment now."[7]

It's not about ignoring hardship. That's just repression in a smart coat. It's about choosing what kind of person you'll be in the middle of it. Wet, maybe. But not undone.

So, next time life veers off-script — your plans unravel, your bike won't start, or someone on the internet is wrong — pause. Ask: *What's happening, and what am I layering on top of it?*

You'll find a strange kind of freedom there. And maybe, even in the rain, a reason to keep riding.

The Problem Is the Path

There's a particular sort of disappointment that comes when life fails to unfold like a brochure. You expect something scenic — progress in a straight line, success on schedule. Instead, you get rain. Or silence. Or an inbox full of things you didn't sign up for.

It's natural to think something's gone wrong. That there's been a clerical error in the divine filing cabinet. But perhaps, as the Stoics suggest, the road isn't broken. It's just the road.

Shakespeare said it best: "There is nothing either good or bad, but thinking makes it so."[8] Hamlet is reflecting on how our perceptions, not the events themselves, create our emotional reactions. In Hamlet's case, he's saying Denmark *shouldn't* feel like a prison – but to him, it does, *because of how he's thinking about it.* It sounds terribly modern for a man who lived without electricity. But there it is: Reality is fine. It's our interpretation that causes trouble.

And, frankly, we're often dramatic about it. A cancelled plan becomes a personal betrayal. A detour becomes evidence that the universe is somehow against us. We treat friction as failure, forgetting that friction is also how we steer, how we brake, how we stay on the bike at all.

I once found myself stuck – literally, figuratively, meteorologically – on a high desert road. The kind of place where the sky feels a bit too large and your own thoughts echo uncomfortably. Life was off-kilter. A few things had come undone. The weather wasn't helping. The sun was blisteringly hot and my satnav and phone had died; I pulled over.

At first, I tried to wait it out, arms folded. But the sun's rays don't negotiate, and when there are no clouds in sight, there's nothing to hide behind except a boulder or two.

Eventually, I stopped sulking and just stood there. The hot wind did nothing to soothe the mood, but somewhere in that stillness came a small clarity: The conditions weren't personal. Only my interpretation was. I looked around and realised – this moment, this place, this discomfort – was entirely of my own making. Every decision I'd taken had led me here. And really, what was so wrong with it? My phone had overheated and given up. The satnav had packed in. I could curse it all – rail against the signal gods and shake my fist at the sky – or I could just let it be. Let *me* be. Alone, yes. Lost, maybe. But surrounded by staggering beauty. The silence. The heat. The impossible vastness. I was here, living and breathing. And for all its flaws, it was a moment of pure privilege – one I'd soon leave behind. So, I stood, and I let it in: the sun's fierce generosity, the sheer force of the planet, the joy of being exactly, perfectly, where I was.

That's when the ride resumed – not in defiance of the sun, but alongside it.

The Stoics would call this *prohairesis* – the choice within, independent of external events.[9] When you choose to breathe, not bite; to wait, not lash out; to respond and not react – that is prohairesis in action. You can't always change the conditions, but you can change the meaning you make of them.

J.K. Rowling, speaking to Harvard graduates, reflected on her own unravelling of failure, grief, and public obscurity. "Rock bottom," she said, "became the solid foundation on which I rebuilt my life."[10] She didn't romanticise suffering. She just didn't waste it. She rode through it with her eyes open.

You don't need to be a global icon to do the same. You just need to be willing to revise the story. Ask yourself: *What if this isn't the wrong road? What if this is just what the terrain looks like when you're changing gear?*

You see, obstacles don't interrupt the journey. They shape it.

Not because life is trying to teach you a lesson, like some divine driving instructor with a clipboard – but because this is simply how roads work. They bend. They roughen. They ask something of you.

And sometimes, when you finally stop resisting, you find the road was never the problem.

You were just holding the handlebars too tight.

Turning Challenges into Opportunities

Have you ever noticed there's a subtle moment inside every hardship? It doesn't always crack the sky or knock you flat. More often, it's quieter than that – a weight that settles in slowly. You don't notice the exact moment things change. You just know the old way of seeing no longer works.

There's a breath. A pause. Something inside says, *This is harder than I wanted.*

And then, if you're paying attention: *Maybe there's something here for me.*

That's the turning point. Not the solution. Not relief. Just a shift in how you're holding it.

The Stoics didn't romanticise adversity. They didn't ask you to enjoy pain or pretend every trial is a blessing. What they offered was a steady compass. Seneca, facing his own challenges during his time, reminded himself: "Difficulties strengthen the mind as labor does the body."[11] In other words: Hardship is framed not as a detour but as the training ground. The 'difficult road' is what makes you capable; it is not something to avoid.

A couple I met on tour recently in Spain – let's call them Angelina and John – spent years building a business. They poured everything into it. Time. Money. Identity. And then, just before launch of a brand-new product, COVID happened and their investors pulled out. The company folded within weeks. The loss wasn't just financial; it was their home and their future that disappeared. It shook their sense of who they were.

Over coffee, John said, "We spent the last decade climbing a mountain. And then we realised we were on the wrong one."

They began to re-evaluate what truly mattered – their values, their identity, the shape of the life they were building. What choices could they make that aligned more deeply with what they believed? How could they create space for the things that actually gave life meaning – family, friendships, time?

This wasn't a moment to slip back into the familiar. It was a rare chance to rebuild from the foundations – to craft something real. They saw how deeply they'd been tethered to a lifestyle that promised everything yet delivered only emptiness. The relentless pursuit of *more* – more success, more stuff, more noise – had narrowed their view like blinders on a horse. It was just easier to keep going than to question the path.

But when that world disappeared, so did the invisible weight it carried. The loss, they realised, wasn't ruin – it was release. What once held them down like a lead anchor had, in falling away, set them free.

They started a brand-new company based on what they saw the world needed, then shifted into advisory work. Not as a fallback – they discovered it lit them up in a way the startup never had. "Losing the company gave us back our life," he told me. Now they can enjoy living in a way they never did before. Part of that new life included travelling to new countries and seeing the world from the saddle of a motorbike.

It's not that the pain disappeared. It didn't. But their relationship with the pain changed. That's the power of a shift in perspective.

Both philosophy and psychology point to the same truth: Difficult experiences can lead to real growth. When people take time to reflect on what they've been through, they often emerge with a stronger sense of meaning, a clearer purpose, and closer relationships – not in spite of the pain, but because of how they worked through it.[12]

But here's the catch: It's not automatic. It's a choice. And it starts with a question. Not "Why me?" Not even "How do I fix this?" But: *What now becomes possible?*

We tend to look at challenges as things to get past – as quickly and cleanly as possible. But if you pause, just for a moment, there's often more waiting beneath the surface. Not a silver lining. A deeper question.

When I left corporate life, it wasn't some dramatic escape. It was quieter than that. A slow erosion. I stopped recognising myself in the mirror. I had a good job, and a steady salary – but something vital was missing. I felt flat. I'd wake up tired. I stopped laughing at things that used to make me laugh. Something was definitely missing.

And then I attended a funeral. A colleague – a Master Mariner, in fact, who'd taken a shore job to be closer to his young family while they grew but whose veins were still running with the salt of the ocean and whose eyes sparkled like sun on the sea when he recounted stories of captaining oil tankers across vast oceans. He'd retired six months earlier with dreams of sailing the world with his wife now that the kids had flown the nest. He died before he ever stepped on the boat.

That grief became a turning point. I didn't know exactly what I wanted, but I knew what I couldn't return to. That moment of pain offered me a map – not with directions, but with permission to begin.

The Quiet Revolution

Sometimes the biggest changes begin without permission. Not from the world, but from your own conscious mind. No agenda. No drama. Just a crack. A moment. Like when the hum of the engine evens out and, for a split second, you hear the deeper vibration of the machine – and in that tone, you feel something more than sound. You feel alignment.

There's a kind of revolution that begins in those moments. But it doesn't feel like a revolution. It feels like brushing your teeth and realising you're gripping the handle too tightly. Or noticing, mid-walk, that your jaw has been clenched for twenty minutes. You loosen your grip. Not to escape the world, but to stop fighting it. You realise: The problem isn't always what's happening – it's how tightly you're holding it.

This is not resignation. This is awareness.

Epictetus called it the one thing we truly own. The inner place where decisions are made – not the surface reactions, but the deeper movements of the self. You can't choose what the road throws at you: crosswinds, slick pavement, or gravel you didn't see coming. But you *can* choose your posture. You can sit up. You can breathe. You can ride differently.

The mistake we make – again and again – is to equate power with control. But on the bike, you learn quickly: The harder you try to control, the rougher the ride. Oversteer, overcorrect, overthink – you end up in a ditch. The smoother ride comes from responsiveness, not rigidity. Awareness, not assumption.

The same is true off the road.

There was a period in my life when everything felt like a test. Every mistake was a referendum on whether I was good enough, smart enough, or worthy. I gripped my own identity like I gripped the handlebars during my first weeks of riding – white-knuckled and terrified. But slowly, I began to notice something. When I allowed for the possibility that I didn't have to know everything, didn't have to prove anything, things didn't fall apart. They got clearer.

Carol Dweck's[13] research calls this a growth mindset, but long before that, it was just called wisdom. It's the shift from "I have to get this right" to "I get to learn something here." From "This shouldn't be happening" to "What now?" Not a change in outcome, but in orientation.

I keep one phrase close when I catch myself spiralling: *What else might be true?* That one question is a gear shift. A recalibration. It opens the hand, loosens the jaw, and brings me back to the ride.

This isn't positive thinking. It's not a spiritual bypass. It's mechanical. Practical. Like adjusting the carburettor. If your mix is off, the engine sputters. If your perception is off, your life sputters. Simply adjust. Don't abandon.

No need to wait for a breakdown to start. Just listen. The road hums. The machine speaks. Somewhere between your breath and the buzz of your thoughts is a whisper: *It doesn't have to be this way.* And maybe that's enough to begin.

Chapter 2

Choose Your Line

"Everything can be taken from a man but one thing: the last of the human freedoms, to choose one's attitude in any given set of circumstances."
— Viktor Frankl

EXISTENTIALISTS SPEAK OFTEN OF freedom — but not the kind that means doing whatever you want and blaming your horoscope, but the quieter, more demanding freedom of choosing how to live when life becomes difficult. When things go wrong — as they often do — it's not the event itself that defines you, but your response to it.

Viktor Frankl understood this well. We cannot control what others say, or how they behave. We cannot dictate the weather, our health, or the road conditions on the day of the ride. But we can decide how we meet these things. And that decision — often made in private, without applause — shapes everything that follows.

In an age obsessed with control, choosing to live honestly, without a perfect script, becomes a kind of quiet rebellion. Sartre put it plainly: "Man is nothing else but what he makes of himself."[14] It's an inconvenient truth. You are the maker and the material, the artist and the error.

Living authentically doesn't require mastery. It asks for sincerity. It means acknowledging what truly matters, and moving toward it — even when the road feels uncertain, or the path is wet with doubt.

Most people aren't choosing. They're drifting — into jobs, into habits, into the long silence of resignation. But the moment you see that the road is yours to shape, the landscape changes. You stop following signs. You begin to steer. You look for roads that stretch you, bend you slightly, and remind you that you're alive.

On the bike, this principle is clear: You're not a passenger — you're the rider.

The road throws everything at you — gravel, rain, blind corners, careless drivers. You can't control the weather, the traffic, or the unpredictable world beyond your visor. But you can choose your line, the path you carve through uncertainty, and focus on what you can influence — your thoughts, your choices, your actions — and accept what you cannot. Seneca put it beautifully, albeit with his choice of a sailing metaphor, not a motorcycling one: "If a man knows not to which port he sails, no wind is favourable."[15] If you don't choose your line – your direction – then no opportunity or external condition will help. You'll drift, reactive instead of deliberate.

The Existential Biker

It was May 2017, the start of my first European tour with a company called Magellan, which I would eventually guide for. I was nervous. *Wobbly*. Afraid of stopping. Afraid of cornering. Afraid of going fast. I wouldn't take the bike above 50 mph on the motorway, which, in touring terms, is roughly the speed of a determined jogger.

And it rained. It rained as if the continent had been saving up for this very week. Not just a drizzle, but a theatrical, all-day soaking. The kind that makes you question your decisions and wonder if, as a Brit, escaping the rain was ever a realistic ambition.

We're often told change takes time. Gradual. Layered. Like sedimentary rock. But I don't buy it. Sometimes, change comes all at once – if the timing is right, if the people around you encourage you and lift you up, or if you simply stop repeating "I can't" and try "I can" instead.

My moment came in the forecourt of a disused petrol station somewhere in the middle of Europe.

I was cold. Ready to pack it in and call it character-building. This touring business clearly wasn't for me. Too hard. Too wet. And too fast.

Then the guide strolled over and explained, in the calm and slightly bored tone of someone who'd done this many times before, how tyres work in the rain. How grip is a function of design, not weather. How water is channelled away by grooves, how the rubber sticks to the road, and – crucially – how none of this was remotely relevant to someone who never went above 50 mph anyway.

But something shifted in me. Maybe it was the look on his face that did it. Because in that moment, I saw myself as *he* saw me – hesitant, unsure, afraid. And the truth hit hard: I *was* behaving like that. He was holding up a mirror I didn't like, reflecting back a version of me I'd never agreed to become.

I thought of the little girl I once was – the one who lost her father and felt completely alone in the world. I remembered the promise I made to her, right there in the school playground. I told her I'd never leave her. That I'd never forget who she was. That we'd face everything the world threw at us without fear. I swore I'd always be her best friend – strong, loyal, unshakable.

And yet here I was, being . . . well, less than that.

I rode out of that forecourt like someone who *meant* it. I found the rest of the gears. I used them – in the rain, no less.

What had changed? Not the weather. Not the road.

Me.

I remembered who I'd promised I would be. I did it for *her*.

And sometimes, all it takes is one moment – one reflection – to change everything.

* * *

This brings us, in a roundabout way, to the question of names. Specifically, The Existential Biker. It sounds like a contradiction – leather jackets and French philosophy, potholes and Søren Kierkegaard. But it's really quite straightforward. Riding a motorcycle demands presence. It demands clarity, courage, and a relationship with reality that's . . . well, less mediated than most. It's rather hard to lie to yourself at 70 mph in a crosswind.

And existentialism, for all its beret-wearing caricature, is fundamentally about choice. Not just the big, sprawling, life-rearranging kinds of choices – but the small ones. The constant ones. The ones that build character, like tiny bricks, over time.

That's why I chose the name. It reflects a way of moving through the world. One hand on the throttle. One eye on the horizon. One foot in the question, "What now?"

Because bike riding, for me, is not just about speed or escape. It's a way of making sense of things. A way of moving with life rather than against it. The road isn't always smooth. Nor is the weather always fine. But within all that unpredictability is the single, unshakable truth: You get to choose how you ride it.

And that is no small thing.

In a world where many choices are made for us – by governments, by algorithms, by circumstance – the one remaining freedom, as Viktor Frankl so precisely observed, is how we respond. That inner space. That flicker of autonomy. That is where our power lives.

To know you have this freedom is the biggest asset you could ever have.

It's the difference between shrinking back from life or leaning, quite literally, into it.

The Stoics called this awareness the dichotomy of control. They taught that life's challenges fall into two categories: what we can control, and what we cannot. Your line on the road is your choice – even if the rain, the potholes, the cars around you are not. Denzel Washington, a stoic at heart, delivered this nugget of wisdom at his commencement speech at Dillard University in 2015: "Don't confuse movement with progress. You can run in place all the time and never get anywhere." Responding with intention, rather than impulse, is its own kind of strength. It's the skill of reading the moment – knowing when to lean in and when to hold steady and not be distracted by things on the periphery

Buddhism offers a similar, well-known teaching known as the two arrows.

The first is pain – the kind that comes with being human. A sudden storm, a sharp loss, a moment of fear. These experiences strike without warning. The second arrow is different. It's the suffering we add through resistance, anger, or the belief that things should be otherwise. Pain may be inevitable, but suffering often isn't. We may not choose the first arrow, but we can choose whether to release the second.

You are not a passenger on this journey. You are the rider – not just in body, but in mind and spirit. You hold the handlebars, but you also hold the power to choose your path through the uncertainty. Each decision, each response, shapes your ride and your life. This freedom to choose your line is your greatest asset.

As you read on, notice the space between what happens and how you respond. That's where the choice lives. Whether you're riding or simply going about your day, look for your line. Take it with intention. Because once you realise that response is yours to shape, fear loses its grip. And what's left is something quieter – something steady enough to ride on.

The Power of Choice in Shaping Your Path

Somewhere near the border with Switzerland, on a mountain pass that had long since stopped being fun,

I found myself stuck behind a dithering campervan in a fog so thick it felt almost curated. Visibility was down to ten feet. My visor was streaked, my fingers were numb, and I was beginning to suspect that the hot chocolate advertised at the top of the pass was a cruel myth, like punctual tradesmen or low-fat croissants.

I had a choice. I could sit there, fuming, teeth chattering, questioning every decision that had led me to this godforsaken incline. Or I could ease past the campervan, hug the right line of the curve, and hope I didn't meet a coach full of Italian pensioners coming the other way. Neither option promised comfort. But dithering – well, that wasn't really an option at all.

We like to imagine that choices, especially important ones, arrive with clarity. They don't. They tend to arrive with damp gloves, low visibility, and no clear answer. But in those moments, something subtle happens. We realise that while we can't control the fog, we can control how we ride through it.

It's not romantic. It's not especially dramatic. It's usually quite mundane. You're cold, you're tired, the road is long, and something within you says: Choose. Go forward. Turn back. Wait. Speak. Stay silent. You choose, and that decision becomes a hinge – often unnoticed – on which your whole path swings.

History is full of hinges – moments when a single decision, made deliberately under pressure, changes the course of everything that follows. Take Winston

Churchill in 1940. Britain stood on a knife-edge. The easier path was to seek peace, appease an overwhelming force, and hope for mercy. But Churchill refused. His choice was a deliberate act rooted in conviction. He understood that retreat might offer immediate relief, but it would surrender the future. His steadfastness shaped not only the war but the world order that followed. That moment was about knowing when to stand firm and when to act with courage – a lesson that echoes far beyond the battlefield.

Then there's Michel de Montaigne, a man of quieter battles. In the 16th century, amid political turmoil and personal doubt, he chose to step away from public life and his career in politics. Instead of chasing power or fame, he turned inward, writing essays that explored what it means to live honestly and thoughtfully. Montaigne's decision to retire wasn't an escape but a deliberate pause – an alignment of his actions with his values. His reflections, written in solitude, continue to influence how we think about self-awareness and human nature centuries later. He showed us that sometimes, the greatest impact comes from standing still long enough to understand yourself, rather than rushing forward.

Both men faced pressure. Both made deliberate choices. Both shaped history – not because they had all the answers, but because they embraced responsibility for their responses.

This is the same wisdom you find when riding a bike through uncertainty or navigating life's unexpected curves. It's about knowing when to push forward and when to hold your ground, all while staying true to what you value. This is what motorcycling, at its best, teaches you. You cannot coast through the Alps on autopilot. The road insists on presence. Each corner demands a decision. And each decision, however small, reinforces the path you're taking – not just geographically, but inwardly.

So no, I didn't pass the campervan. I waited. I sipped from a lukewarm flask and the fog lifted eventually, as fogs do. And I rode on, not triumphant, but steady – aware, once again, that the power to choose, especially when things are uncertain, is the beginning of every honest path.

Accepting Responsibility for Your Responses

Let's talk about responsibility – not the tedious kind you dread on Monday mornings, but the kind that quietly shifts your whole outlook. You and I don't get to control much of what happens to us. People will behave in ways you'd rather they didn't. The road will be slippery just when you least expect it. But what you do with those things – that's yours, utterly and irrevocably.

Taking responsibility for your response is not about burdening yourself with blame or imagining you're the centre of a cosmic drama. It's far simpler – and far more powerful. It's about recognising that between the event and your reaction, there's a space. That space is your domain. And in it, you hold choice.

Marcus Aurelius advised himself to remember that he was "an actor in a play"[16] and that the play itself was brief. If you see your life that way, responsibility isn't a weight – it's your role, your improvisation in the scene. You can't choose the script, but you can choose how you deliver your lines.

When you accept responsibility for your reactions, you no longer feel tossed about by circumstance. You become the steady hand on the handlebars. That steadiness – that quiet command – is what carries you forward, no matter what the weather or the road throws at you.

Knowing When to Act and When to Stand Firm

There is a peculiar art to knowing when to act and when to stand firm – a skill every rider learns, whether they're navigating the serpentine roads of the Alps or the metaphorical curves of everyday life. It is a kind of dance with circumstance, not unlike knowing when to ease off the throttle or when to lean deeper into a corner. Too much haste, and you risk disaster; too much hesitation, and the moment slips past, leaving you stranded.

I recall a story from the 1920s about T.E. Lawrence – better known as Lawrence of Arabia – who was as much a master of timing as he was of desert warfare. Lawrence understood that sometimes the boldest action was inaction, holding ground rather than charging ahead. He wrote in his memoir *Seven Pillars of Wisdom* that "all men dream: but not equally. Those who dream by night in the dusty recesses of their minds wake in the day to find that it was vanity: but the dreamers of the day are dangerous men."[17] His point: Discernment about when to move and when to hold fast is critical – dreaming by day means acting with purpose, not blindly.

The Stoics offer us a kindred wisdom. Epictetus[18] taught that the world offers events as it will; it is our judgements and actions that are ours to command. This doesn't mean reckless passivity. It means careful engagement. There's a moment when the smart rider eases off, lets the road come to them, and waits for clarity. And there's a moment when hesitation is a luxury you cannot afford.

This balance between action and stillness is also reflected in the martial art of Aikido. The practitioner neither attacks nor resists force outright but blends with it, redirecting energy with grace and timing. As the British-American philosopher Alan Watts noted, "The art of living . . . is neither careless drifting on the one hand nor fearful clinging to the past on the other. It consists in being sensitive to each moment, in regarding it as utterly new and unique, in having the mind open and wholly receptive."[19] Sensitivity to timing – knowing when to move and when to hold – is the heartbeat of both martial arts and mindful living.

In our lives, as on the road, indecision can be its own hazard. But so can rashness. Learning to distinguish the moments requires presence, experience, and a kind of calm awareness. It's the quiet confidence that comes from knowing you don't have to act on every impulse, but also that when action is needed, hesitation is a luxury.

The next time you face a fork in your path – literal or metaphorical – ask yourself: *Is this a moment to stand firm or to move?* And trust that wisdom often arrives not in the noise of action but in the pause between.

Chapter 3

Amor Fati – Love of Fate

"That one wants nothing to be different, not forward, not backwards, not in all eternity. Not merely bear what is necessary, still less conceal it . . . but love it."
— Nietzsche

AMOR FATI. IT SOUNDS like something a Roman emperor might grumble over a tepid goblet of wine, doesn't it? But it means "love of fate". Not just endure the cards you're dealt, or grimly shuffle along pretending it's all fine, but truly, deeply love the whole mess – the good, the bad, and the plain bewildering. Friedrich Nietzsche[20], the philosopher who rarely minced words, captured this idea vividly when he wrote of wanting nothing in life to be different and of loving necessity itself rather than merely tolerating it. That's the challenge – to embrace life's bumps as if they were old friends rather than unwelcome guests.

When I first lined up to race on the Bonneville Salt Flats, I wasn't nervous in the usual adrenaline-pumped way. Instead, I was calm, oddly serene. I'd heard the conditions were brutal – two of the three lanes closed after heavy rains, salt sludge turning the track into a treacherous Slip 'n' Slide. A rookie rider with zero salt experience should have been a mess of nerves and doubt. Yet, a friend gave me advice that shifted everything: "Accept that you may not make it. Accept your fate, wholly and unconditionally. Do a deal with yourself – and then it's FLAME ON."

This wasn't passive resignation. It was active love for the situation as it stood. I made peace with the possibility of failure before I even kicked the throttle. The track, the weather, even the threat of disaster – I welcomed them all. Not because I was fearless, but because I'd chosen to ride *with* fate, not against it.

Stoicism urges us to "love the hand that fate deals you."[21] To find freedom not in bending the world to our will but in bending ourselves to the world's will, in gratitude for whatever arises. This is radical. It means that even hardship and suffering – the potholes and detours on life's ride – can be gifts if we learn to welcome them.

Amor fati calls for full presence – meeting each moment with clarity and openness and trusting that every twist in the road carries its own lesson. Imagine a rider who doesn't fight the wind but leans into it, who knows the path will throw curveballs but chooses to love the journey anyway. That rider is free.

This chapter is about how you can ride with fate, not against it. How to find gratitude in the grit. How to transform hardship into a companion rather than an enemy. And how, sometimes, the only choice that really matters is to say: *This is exactly what I needed.*

Developing Gratitude for All Experiences

Gratitude has, let's be honest, suffered a bit of an image problem. It tends to appear on fridge magnets and wellness podcasts, often in the company of herbal tea and soothing flutes. But to the Stoics, gratitude wasn't a mood – it was a discipline. Less scented candle, more toolkit. Less emotional glow, more mental grip.

Marcus Aurelius, who wasn't exactly lounging in spas during his time as Emperor (what with plagues, border wars, and a stroppy Senate), put it plainly: "Receive without pride, let go without attachment."[22] It's not a motto for passive resignation. It's an approach to life where you meet each event with an open hand – not a clenched fist. A flat tyre. A missed train. A rainstorm on the only day you left the waterproofs behind. These aren't interruptions. They're invitations.

Think of it like this: You're halfway through a ride when the bike coughs, splutters, and dies. At first, there's the usual muttering and expletives. You kick a stone. You curse the weather, the fuel, yourself. But then something shifts. A fellow rider pulls over. You talk. Tools come out. The problem gets fixed – or it doesn't – but the story changes. The breakdown becomes the bond. And when you look back later, it's not the smooth ride you remember. It's this.

Epictetus put it more elegantly: "Don't seek for everything to happen as you wish it would, but rather wish that everything happens as it actually will."[23] In other words, stop arguing with reality. Life isn't here to match your itinerary.

This isn't to say we should start applauding every misfortune like an overzealous life coach. No one enjoys soggy socks or a seized clutch. But what if gratitude isn't about liking the moment, but simply being willing to learn from it?

The Stoics didn't preach gratitude for hardship – they practised gratitude through it. That's a subtle but crucial distinction. It's not masochism. It's clarity.

I once made a rookie error and filled my tank with Diesel at a remote fuel station in Germany. I'd been riding with a friend I'd just met in Italy where we'd been riding as part of the Women Rider's World Relay. We were exhausted, we had to get to Berlin that evening, it was late in the afternoon and had started to rain, and we still had another couple of hundred miles to go. We called for help and eventually a guy in a truck came and took us to his garage. We had such an interesting conversation and shared so much of each of our unique perspectives on philosophy, country, and life that when we got to the garage, I was almost sad.

I thanked the guy who'd rescued us at the time, but I've thanked that moment even more often since. Not because I want to repeat it (unfortunately I did more recently – but that's another story), but because it taught me something I couldn't have learned on a dry road with a full tank. It taught me about how, in the middle of even unwanted experiences, something true and of value can come about. In this case, how we can become richer when we venture to share our humanity with strangers.

Gratitude, in this deeper sense, doesn't demand that you enjoy every moment. It just asks that you don't waste it.

Next time something goes sideways – bike, life, both – pause. Ask yourself: What's here for me, even now? Not in a self-help kind of way. In a real, grounded, grown-up way.

Because sometimes, the day you break down is the day you really begin to ride.

How Accepting Fate Leads to Peace

"Amor fati: let that be my love henceforth! I do not want to wage war against what is ugly. I do not want to accuse; I do not even want to accuse those who accuse. Looking away shall be my only negation. And all in all and on the whole: some day I wish to be only a Yes-sayer." – Nietzsche

Nietzsche's call to "be only a Yes-sayer" feels like a radical act in a world that constantly tempts us to say no – to resist, to rail, to fight what is uncomfortable or unjust. *Amor fati* asks us not just to tolerate what life throws at us, but to embrace it fully. To stop waging war on reality's bumps and bruises, and instead welcome them as part of the ride. It's an active, soulful surrender that brings peace.

Imagine you're walking through a dense forest on a winding trail. The path twists unexpectedly, roots jut out where you least expect them, and the light shifts constantly through the trees. Your first instinct might be frustration or impatience with the obstacles. But what if, instead, you chose to say "yes" to the uneven ground? To the surprises around every bend? To the forest exactly as it is, not as you wished it to be?

You stop resisting the challenges and start moving with them, finding quiet freedom in embracing the journey as it comes.

"Make the best use of what is in your power, and take the rest as it happens."[24] The rest — the things you cannot control — are the very fabric of fate. Resisting them only drains energy and breeds unrest. Accepting them opens space for peace.

Here's a little-known gem: In the March 1968 issue of *Playboy* — yes, the magazine you might not expect to find philosophy in — Stanley Kubrick offered a thoughtful interview about life's meaning. He noted that life's ultimate indifference — neither hostile nor kind — can be terrifying. Yet, if we make peace with this indifference, we can create meaning within it. Kubrick said that while children start with pure wonder, growing up brings awareness of death, decay, and chaos, which can erode joy. But if you are strong and lucky, you emerge anew, shaping a lasting purpose despite life's absurdities.

This reflects the Stoic teaching that true peace arises not from escaping life's challenges, but from embracing them fully. As Marcus Aurelius put it, "Love the hand that fate deals you and play it as your own."[25] Picture your life as a motorcycle ride — not a smooth, easy path, but a wild journey filled with potholes, unexpected detours, and sudden changes in weather. The rider who embraces their fate stays steady amid the turmoil, understanding that the bumps aren't barriers to overcome but part of the road itself.

When I lined up to race on the salt flats, the place was as unforgiving as any philosophical test. The salt was wet, the track uncertain. A friend told me to accept my fate, to fully own whatever outcome came, good or bad, and then ride like hell. To accept my fate was not to surrender, but to be set free. It cleared the fog of fear and let me ride with clarity.

Amor fati invites us to say "yes" to life exactly as it is, finding peace not in spite of fate, but through it. This mindset shapes both rider and life – not by seeking control, but by embracing grace.

On Suffering and Hardship

Suffering has a way of arriving when the kettle's just boiled and you've settled into a chair. It doesn't knock. It just barges in, sits opposite you, and expects a conversation. Often, a long one.

The Stoics were rather pragmatic about hardship. They didn't dress it up or explain it away with cosmic promises. They didn't say, "Everything happens for a reason." That's too neat, and life is rarely neat. Instead, they asked a better question: "What will you do with this?"

When the pandemic arrived, the world slowed down and sped up in the wrong places. Loss came – jobs, people, routines. We were forcibly reacquainted with silence, stillness, and uncertainty. That global pause exposed a truth the Stoics knew well: Control is limited, but response is sovereign.

Epictetus, born a slave who later began teaching philosophy after gaining his freedom, taught that we must distinguish between what we can control and what we cannot. The rest is wasted effort – like trying to command the weather or reason with pigeons. You can't stop the rain, but you can wear a better coat. You can't change a loss, but you can decide what kind of person you become in the aftermath.

True engagement means meeting reality on its own terms with emotional honesty and strength. Instead of pretending suffering is noble, you stop insisting it shouldn't exist.

Marcus Aurelius, in contrast to Epictetus, was a Roman emperor, military commander, and part-time insomniac philosopher. His reign was marked by plagues, wars, and palace intrigue, yet he wrote, "If it's endurable, then endure it. If it's unendurable . . . then stop complaining. Your destruction will mean its end as well."[26] It sounds harsh until you realise what he's offering: a choice. Even in your bleakest moments, you remain the architect of your attitude.

You can see this in more everyday stories too. I was once riding with a friend who, having broken down mid-tour in Romania, spent the day helping a local farmer repair a tractor instead. His plans had collapsed, but his spirit hadn't. "It's all part of the ride," he shrugged. That's *amor fati* in action – loving what happens, even when it smells of diesel and failed expectations.

We live in a culture that encourages us to fix, hack, or optimise everything. But some things aren't meant to be fixed. They're meant to be faced. With grit. With grace. Possibly with a biscuit.

The Stoic view is that hardship doesn't make you a victim. It makes you a participant in a very old play. The script is full of surprise scenes, but your performance? That's yours to shape.

Aligning Actions with Values

You don't need a dramatic life overhaul to live like a Stoic. You don't need to swap your house for a cave or start quoting Marcus Aurelius at office meetings – though, admittedly, it's a good way to shorten them. What Stoicism suggests, instead, is something quieter. Something durable. That you begin to act in line with what you claim to believe.

It's the philosophical equivalent of putting your tools back where you found them. Nothing flashy. Just a quiet integrity between the inner and the outer.

The Stoics weren't terribly interested in showy declarations. Seneca warned that "philosophy isn't a parlour trick."[27] It was supposed to shape how you lived – not just how you sounded after a glass of red.

So, the real question becomes: What do you value, and what small daily acts reflect that?

You say you value kindness. Did you offer it today?

You say you care about honesty. Were you, even when it was inconvenient?

You say you want to live with purpose. Did your choices point that way – even slightly?

The Stoics didn't expect perfection. But they did expect effort. Even if it was mostly uphill.

And it is mostly uphill.

Robert Pirsig in *Zen and the Art of Motorcycle Maintenance* reminds us that quality isn't an act – it's a way of being.[28] He wasn't talking about expensive oil changes. He meant a way of noticing. A way of bringing your full self to what you're doing. Whether that's making tea or mending a puncture. Quality, in this sense, is a moral stance.

In the same way, *amor fati* invites us to do more than just endure the road ahead. It asks us to lean into it. Not to grimace through it, but to say – somewhat improbably – "Yes. Even this."

Even the flat tyre.

Even the wrong turn.

Even the waiting.

Because if you can accept those, not as glitches but as features of the ride, you'll travel lighter. You'll stop trying to bend the world into your shape. You'll start aligning yourself, instead, with what matters.

There's a kind of peace that comes from this. Not the beach holiday sort of peace, but the deep-seated stillness that comes from living without contradiction. When your actions echo your principles. When you stop splitting yourself into who you are and who you mean to be.

PART TWO

INTENTION

You don't always know the destination, but you feel when the ride starts to mean something.

Intention lives in small things — how you start the day, where your energy goes, what you protect. It's not found in some big revelation. It's in the decision to pay attention. These pages ask quiet questions: What pulls you forward? What are you choosing, even when you say nothing?

Chapter 4

Memento Mori – Remember You Must Die

"Let us prepare our minds as if we'd come to the very end of life. Let us postpone nothing."
— Seneca

The road in North Wales had climbed steadily all afternoon until it didn't anymore. No warning signs. Just an abrupt stop at the edge of the world, where land gives way to sky. A few sheep watched me like disapproving aunties.

I lifted my visor, and suddenly the wind touched my cheeks, and with it came a question I hadn't planned to ask: *What if this were the last ride?*

Not in a dramatic, crash-and-flames kind of way. Just . . . the last. No encore. No rerun. What would I regret? What would I wish I'd done?

It's strange how death, when considered without panic, doesn't feel heavy. It just feels very, very clarifying. Emails, the to-do list, and whatever that argument was about yesterday – none of it matters. What remains is simpler. The question that doesn't flinch: *Am I living in a way that feels honest?*

Seneca advised us to live each day as if it were a complete life. "Let us postpone nothing," he wrote. "Let us balance life's account daily."[29] It sounds like something my accountant might say – only with fewer togas and more spreadsheets. But Seneca wasn't talking about finances. He was reminding us that life is finite. That death isn't a distant abstraction but something intimately close.

I've known that for a long time. My father died when I was thirteen. My mother followed just over a decade later. And ten years after that, the father of my children was gone, too.

I didn't need a philosopher to tell me that life is fragile. It's been clear to me since I was a girl – not in theory, but in practice.

So, when the Master Mariner we mentioned earlier died just months into his long-anticipated retirement, I wasn't shocked by the fact of death itself. But something about that funeral . . . pushed me over the edge.

It was a plain service, with a few touches that paid homage to his seafaring career. A quiet country church. I sat next to a colleague – one with a full pack of tissues, thank God – because I cried like a child. Not a dignified dab of the eye. Full, uncontrollable sobs. My nose ran, my eyes puffed up, and no matter how much I tried to rein it in, I couldn't stop. The tissues ran out eventually and I remember piecing together the damp, soggy remains in my lap in the hope they would soak up just one more outpouring.

I was a little embarrassed, if I'm honest. He wasn't family. We weren't even close friends. And yet, something in me broke. Or maybe it opened. What undid me wasn't just his death – it was the life he didn't get to finish. The dream that never sailed. The joy postponed one season too long.

That day became a catalyst. Something momentous shifted inside me. I stopped saying someday. I booked my flights for the first leg of my adventure. Took a sabbatical instead of resigning. It wasn't brave. It was necessary.

That's the spirit of this chapter.

You don't need to quit your job or move to Patagonia. But you do need to ask: *What would I do differently if I remembered this all ends?*

Would you be more honest? Kinder? Braver? Would you still wait to say what you really mean?

We ride differently when we know it's the last lap. Tighter lines. Fewer distractions. More attention to the view. Less to prove.

Death, paradoxically, brings life into sharper focus. It's the edge that gives the ride shape. So ask yourself: *How would I live if I stopped postponing?*

And then, maybe, start living like that.

Death as a Compass

You don't need a near-death experience to wake up. But it does help.

Let's not be dramatic. This isn't about scaring you. We've had quite enough of that, thank you, between the news and bathroom scales that keep adding numbers we never agreed to. No – this chapter is not here to depress you. It's here to wake you up, gently, like a friend nudging your arm with a good cup of tea and a raised eyebrow.

The Stoics were admirably calm about death. Rather British, actually. No panic. No fuss. Just an acknowledgment that it's there, always waiting in the wings, cue in hand. Interestingly, the Romans had a habit at their victory feasts – just as the garlands were being handed out and egos inflated like overconfident soufflés, a servant would whisper in the ear of the triumphant general: *Memento mori*. It wasn't a threat. It was an invitation: *Remember you must die – so live accordingly.* Don't waste time pretending you're immortal. You're not.

There's a modern echo in Steve Jobs's now-famous words at Stanford: "Remembering that you are going to die is the best way I know to avoid the trap of thinking you have something to lose."[30]

There it is again – not fear, but focus.

There's a curious thing that happens when you ride with death in your mirror.

You notice more.

The angle of sunlight across the tarmac. The particular sound your tyres make on wet gravel. The way your thoughts settle when there's no phone, no emails – just the road and the question humming beneath it all: *Am I living the life I am meant to live?*

In *Meditations* 4.47, Marcus Aurelius reminds himself that death can come at any moment, and that this awareness should guide how we live – shaping our actions, words, and thoughts with urgency and purpose. Not grim. Just plain Roman common sense. If it could all end by teatime, are you really going to spend your morning arguing over a kitchen refit?

Modern psychology has caught up with this ancient wisdom. Bronnie Ware, an Australian palliative nurse, spent years listening to the final words of the dying. The most common regret reported by the dying, Ware writes, was: "I wish I'd had the courage to live a life true to myself, not the life others expected of me."[31] Not more money. Not better abs. Just truth.

And truth, it seems, is harder to locate than we'd like to admit. Martha Beck, in her brilliant work *Finding Your Own North Star*, talks about two selves inside each of us: the *Essential Self*, who we were before the world told us who to be, and the *Social Self*, who learned to fit in, comply, people-please.[32] The Essential Self wants to sing badly in the car, wear red trousers, or move to the coast and write poetry. The Social Self files VAT returns, joins the PTA, and wears navy.

Beck uses the metaphor of the caterpillar. To become a butterfly, it doesn't just grow wings. It dissolves. Fully. Inside the chrysalis, everything melts. Then – strangely – it reconstitutes. But to be reborn, it must first struggle, *really* struggle, to break free from the shell. That exertion isn't just symbolic. It's critical. Skip the fight, and the wings won't form properly. Without resistance, they stay soft, underdeveloped. The harder the effort, the stronger the wings – and the better the chance of survival.

It's a bit like life. Transformation is messy. And hard. But it beats staying a caterpillar because you're scared of what the wings might cost.

Your journey doesn't need to involve deserts or mountain passes. Maybe it's joining a choir. Going back to school. Learning Italian for no practical reason at all. Maybe it's telling someone the truth. Or walking away from something that no longer fits.

Because when you live with death in your mirror, you lean into the corners. You don't waste a mile.

And you stop apologising for wanting what you want.

So yes – prepare for the end. Not in a fire-and-brimstone way, but in the quiet, Stoic manner of someone who knows that all this is fleeting. That there's no refund for unused days. As Basil Fawlty once put it:

> Zhoom!
> What was that?
> That was your life, Mate!
> Oh, that was quick. Do I get another?
> Sorry, Mate. That's your lot.[33]

The Time Warp

Time itself seems to warp as we get older. When we're young, summers stretch on forever. By midlife, they're over before the lawn has a chance to grow properly. The psychologist William James suggested that the speed of time is linked to novelty: The more routine your life becomes, the quicker it passes. So perhaps the answer is not just to live longer, but to *live newer*.

And there's science to back this up. Our brains, ever efficient, don't bother storing every repeated experience in full detail – they compress them. Drive the same route to work a thousand times, and your mind won't keep a thousand memories. Instead, it builds a kind of "template" – a schema – that smooths them all into one. The music. The weather. The red car in front. Gone.

Psychologists call this semantic compression – the brain's way of conserving energy by summarising the familiar.[34] It's closely tied to our use of schemas, mental shortcuts that help us function but also cause memory to blur repeated events.[35] That's why a single unusual day can seem longer and more vivid than an entire week of routine.

So if time feels like it's slipping through your fingers, one antidote is simple: Do something new. Break the pattern. New experiences – no matter how small – expand your sense of time. Take a different route home. Speak to a stranger. Try a dish you can't pronounce. Novelty anchors you to the present and stretches time wide open.

Most of us live as if we have a bottomless supply of mornings. We make grand plans for "someday," as if the gods had promised us a fixed ninety-year lease with optional extensions. But they haven't. And as uncomfortable as that truth is, it's the very thing that can snap us awake.

There's a strange thing that happens when you start contemplating death with any seriousness. Like cleaning the garage. You start to see what's worth keeping.

Psychologists call this "mortality salience" – the awareness, conscious or not, that we're going to die. And when we face that fact, something surprising happens: We start caring less about petty anxieties and more about what truly matters. Research shows that this kind of awareness, if held with perspective, can increase gratitude, presence, and purpose.[36]

But of course, the Stoics got there two thousand years earlier – with fewer acronyms and far better beards. I've found this to be true not just in theory, but in the quiet mechanics of everyday life. When someone you love dies, or you're confronted with a brush of your own mortality, there's an internal rearrangement. What felt urgent yesterday – replies, errands, social standing – suddenly feels faintly ridiculous. You look at your to-do list and wonder why "organise sock drawer" was ever considered high priority.

Which brings us to Albert Camus, a man who could find meaning in absurdity and still manage to smoke stylishly while doing it. In *The Myth of Sisyphus*, he wrote: "There is but one truly serious philosophical problem, and that is suicide."[37] That may sound bleak over breakfast, but his point was existential, not morbid. Camus wasn't endorsing suicide – he was rejecting it. He saw it as a surrender, a way of escaping the absurd rather than facing it. To him, the courageous act was not to bow out, but to stay – to live fully in a world that makes no ultimate sense, and still insist on creating meaning anyway. That defiance, that insistence on living *in spite of*, is what gives us dignity.

If life has no inherent meaning, then we are free – *gloriously free* – to create it ourselves. The absurdity gives us agency.

Victor Frankl, who endured the unendurable in a concentration camp, came to a similar yet more compassionate conclusion: Meaning arises from *responsibility*.[38] Not to others necessarily, but to ourselves and to our unlived lives. He wrote, "Life is never made unbearable by circumstances, but only by lack of meaning and purpose."[39] The man who lost everything still insisted we had the power to choose how to face the day. I find that humbling. And also a little inconvenient – because it means we can no longer blame the world for our inertia.

A friend of mine, Claire Elsdon, once gave me a copy of Frankl's book, *Man's Search for Meaning*. She'd originally bought it for herself but handed it to me first – saying she'd noticed my tendency to bring a philosophical angle to just about any conversation, even when buying papayas at a roadside stall. I was in Tanzania at the time, volunteering with Pikilily, the organisation Claire founded to promote motorcycle and road safety. In Tanzania, road traffic fatalities are nearly double the global average, so education on even the simplest safety practices can have a profound impact, especially for children.

While I was there, Claire was developing a new community-based format of the initiative – MJ Piki

– a locally led program training women to ride and repair motorcycles. It opened a path and gave them the skills to earn a living as delivery riders or motorcycle taxi drivers. It was, in every sense, purpose in motion, a living example of Frankl's belief that even in difficult places, we can choose to serve something meaningful.

Biologically, our relationship with death shifts as we age. Hormones ebb. Roles change. Our children grow up. We begin to ask, consciously or not: What have I done with my time? What will I leave behind? These are not questions for retirement. They are questions for *today*. Right now, this minute, while you still have the strength to climb a hill, phone a friend, book a ticket, write a sentence, or say *I forgive you*. Because a second alive at twenty-five is worth the same as one at seventy-five. The currency doesn't change – only your attention to it does. That's the real cost of ignoring death. Not that it comes – but that we sleepwalk until it does.

So remember death, not to fear it, but to live better. Not to dread the clock ticking down, but to hear it as a steady rhythm: reminding you, quietly but firmly, to dance. There's also a psychological reason to live urgently: *Terror Management Theory*. It sounds more alarming than it is. The idea is that when we're aware of our mortality – even just faintly – we shift our focus. We care less about status and more about what matters. Studies show people reminded of death become more generous, more grateful, and more likely to seek meaning.[40]

That existential awareness doesn't need to be morbid. It can be motivating. When you remember you won't live forever, you stop putting off the life you actually want. You're more likely to speak up, take the trip, say the difficult truth.

Because time perception and mortality are tightly bound. If you want life to feel longer, make it deeper. Fill it with people you love, work that matters, and moments that make you forget to check your phone.

Each day isn't just a page – it's a chance. You get to decide what story it tells.

Living Each Day with Urgency and Purpose

After the shock of my colleague's funeral, I knew something had to change. I didn't want to sleepwalk through life anymore – but like many people, I wasn't sure what "more" looked like. I wanted adventure, yes, but what kind? What shape did joy take now?

So I bought a giant self-stick A1 flipchart pad and stuck it to the wall in my kitchen. My only instruction to myself: Draw what brings you joy. Every time I passed it, I added to it. The flipchart grew like a mutant spider plant – messy, tangled, and weirdly alive. First came an elephant (I wanted to ride one). Then Australia, with a train slicing down the middle. A sketch of the Panama Canal – something I'd always found awe-inspiring from my time in the maritime world. A motorbike. A sailboat. Bright flashes of yearning, scribbled in colour and ink.

I realised I couldn't do everything – not with a new grandson, Teddy, back home. But I could thread a few together. So I booked a flight to Las Vegas and mapped out a journey: Ride a lipstick-red 1000cc Indian Scout through Death Valley, Yosemite, and the Pacific Coast Highway. Then fly to Panama and walk beside the Canal, which was being widened at the time. I caught one of the first massive vessels transiting the locks – a moment that thrilled the maritime nerd in me. From there, I flew to Guadeloupe, where I joined a sailboat as crew. I'd recently earned my Competent Crew qualification, and crossing the Atlantic via Bermuda and New York sounded like an incredible adventure. So I did it.

Sailing was magnificent in its own way – expansive, technical, elegant. There were nights on the ocean when the blackness was all-consuming. I've never seen so many stars in my life. As someone who's loved astronomy ever since I first heard Carl Sagan utter the word "billions" on *Cosmos*, it was desperately life-affirming. Transcendent.

Some nights, when the wind was low and the sea gently slapped against the hull, I'd find myself on deck with one particular crewmate – a Cornishman with the voice of a cathedral. He'd sing these old folk songs into the dark. His rendition of "The Galloway Shawl" still haunts me – beautiful, aching, timeless. That night, under the stars, hearing that song, something welled up inside me. I told him how much it meant to me. He just smiled, quietly pleased to know it had landed.

And then there were nights when the sea rose up like a threat – black, muscular, alive. I gripped the edge of the boat and felt my smallness, my breath tight in my chest, my pulse hammering at my neck. I felt astonishingly alive. Death felt closer on those nights than ever before – but then, so did life.

But looking back now, it wasn't the stars or the sea that changed me – it was what came just before.

None of it had been easy. I hadn't sat on a bike over 125cc in twenty-four years. I had a license, yes, but very little recent experience – and certainly not with long-distance touring in a desert. But off I went anyway.

On that first stretch into Death Valley, I romanticised it far too much. Within hours, I was crying in my helmet. The heat was savage. I got so dehydrated I nearly passed out. The wind knocked over my pride, my ego, and nearly the bike. I gave up in my head half a dozen times that day

That's when Spider appeared.

He was a stocky guy with a grin like mischief and the calmest presence I'd ever met. Turns out he'd been a Navy diver and bomb disposal specialist. Nothing rattled him. And that unshakable energy had a calming effect that I'm convinced got me through. He spotted my pale face and sweaty forehead, handed me two bottles of water, and said, "You're dehydrated. I'm not moving 'til you drink these."

Then he told me to ride at the back with him and his mates. "That's where the fun is," he said. "We're like the naughty kids at the back of the class."

A couple more times, I pulled over and admitted I didn't think I could carry on. Spider just looked at me, steady as a rock, and said, "You *can* do this. As my gran used to say – *a faint heart never fucked a crocodile.*"

And somehow, I did.

We climbed from one hundred feet below sea level to over seven thousand feet, ending the day in Mammoth Lakes. I was still wearing full safety gear despite the desert heat – too scared not to – and by the time we reached the Sierra Nevada mountains, there was snow on the ground and skiers gliding past. It was surreal. Exhausting. And completely life-altering.

I was woefully underprepared. Slow. Shaky. But I made it. And more than that, I found something I hadn't expected: the motorcycling community. People who cheered, encouraged, handed me water, and made me laugh when I wanted to cry. That was the day I fell in love with motorcycles – not just the machines, but the humans that come with them.

None of it was heroic. I wasn't rich, retired, or especially brave.

I was just . . . awake.

Three months later, when I returned home, I remember sitting quietly, and thinking: *That was incredible. That was mine.*

You don't need to cross continents. One of the most liberating rides I've ever taken was a bicycle trip from London to Brighton. Not exotic. Not far. But it was a promise kept to myself. It was a mini-adventure, shared with a few thousand other folks, and I loved every moment. Even when I had to get off and push the bike to the top of the South Downs. It didn't matter – I was in good company. An ordinary day, a novel experience that pulled me out of the theoretical and into the real.

Living with urgency doesn't mean quitting your job and moving to the Andes (unless you really want to). It means recognising that your deepest values – connection, creativity, movement, peace – don't belong in a "someday" folder. They belong in your diary now. As the Stoics reminded us daily, to delay what matters is to gamble with a currency we cannot refund.

Epictetus, ever clear-eyed, wrote: "I cannot escape death, but at least I can escape the fear of it."[41] Not because death is a threat, but because it's a teacher.

Marcus Aurelius reminded himself in *Meditations* that death "is nature's way of cleansing"[42] and that we should keep it near, like a compass.

And what happens when we do? Well, we stop waiting. We give fewer damns about impressing the neighbours. We ask better questions. We measure success in joy, not metrics. We don't need to be extraordinary, just present.

There's enormous liberation in accepting impermanence. It untethers you from the false belief that life will start when you're thinner, richer, more organised. Life doesn't wait. Nor should we.

So ask yourself today – not in a self-help sort of way, but as someone standing in the middle of their one wild and fleeting life – what would you do if you stopped waiting? What vow would you make if you truly believed the time was now?

And what, for heaven's sake, are you waiting for?

The Freedom of Finitude

Of course, retiring early and galloping off into the sunset on a classic motorbike isn't in the cards for most people. Life has its own list of non-negotiables – mortgages, dependants, dodgy boilers. But what I've come to believe, with as much certainty as one can muster while wearing a crash helmet in Death Valley, is that adventure isn't the luxury of the free or the wealthy. It's the mindset of the willing.

I broke a land speed record over a single weekend at my second race meet. No pit crew, no sponsors. The bike cost £1,250 on eBay and, truthfully, I could've sold it for the same amount afterwards. It wasn't about resources. It was about resolve. My first big trip didn't require quitting my job – it just required a well-timed sabbatical and a willingness to look a little foolish.

The Stoics would probably nod politely at this point, then ask what took me so long. Seneca wrote that "we suffer more in imagination than in reality."[43] Most of our barriers are internal. Fear dressed up as logic. Waiting for the perfect moment, which, as you've likely noticed, never actually arrives.

So, if you're waiting for a sign, this might be it. Say yes to your truth. Not the loud, showy version – the quiet one that tugs at you when things go still. Whether it's walking the Camino, learning to dance, or mending a strained friendship, these are all declarations that life matters now.

You can reflect on mortality without dressing in black or reading gravestones. You can ask, each morning: *If this were it, how would I show up?* It doesn't need to be dramatic. Just honest.

Because the real affirmation is this: It's never too early, or too late, to start living as if your days count.

They do.

Chapter 5

Stillness in Motion

"The stillness in stillness is not the real stillness; only when there is stillness in movement does the universal rhythm manifest."
— Bruce Lee

CLOSE YOUR EYES AND imagine for a moment: London traffic is in full, unapologetic swing. Horns, sirens, lorries arguing with bicycles. A man in a Range Rover is shouting at a pedestrian who may or may not be deaf. Amid it all, a rider snakes through the jam – a single lane between the lanes. The bike doesn't roar. It hums. She doesn't flinch, doesn't check her phone, doesn't care about the meeting she's late for. She is still. In motion. Moving, but anchored. The world blurs around her. She's present.

This chapter is about that moment.

It's a paradox, I admit. Movement creating stillness sounds like something a particularly smug yoga teacher might say just before trying to sell you essential oils. But there's truth in it, the Stoics were masters of this principle: that serenity is not found by escaping life, but by engaging with it fully – and choosing how to respond.

"Nowhere," Marcus Aurelius said, "can man find a quieter or more untroubled retreat than in his own soul." He wrote most of his *Meditations* in military camps, probably while listening to swords being sharpened.

He meant that stillness comes from how you direct your attention, not where your body happens to be.

Bruce Lee put it with a bit more flair. Stillness in stillness is easy. Anyone can be calm when nothing is happening. But real stillness – real presence – is when you're in the middle of life's storm and you don't flinch.

Motorcycling, curiously, demands this. You don't ride distracted. If you do, you won't for long. The ride forces awareness of wind, weight, movement, gear, and the car that didn't see you. It's not optional mindfulness. It's survival. But somewhere in that hyper-attention, the chatter quiets. The mind goes still. You experience total immersion in what you're doing, time slowing down, awareness heightening. The self dissolves. Only the moment remains.

Riding is meditation on two wheels. It's why I have friends – hard-boiled, mechanically minded, allergic-to-candlelight-dinners types – who say riding is the only time they feel sane. One calls his bike his "mobile therapist". Another says the engine noise "drowns out the nonsense". I know what they mean.

And it turns out, the science agrees. A 2019 study by UCLA's Semel Institute found that motorcycling reduced cortisol by 28% and increased alertness and focus, similar to light exercise.[44] Your brain, when riding, isn't overloaded. It's refined. Like clearing clutter from a desk. Space emerges. Thought becomes precision.

Stillness is not sitting in silence. Stillness is clarity.

Of course, this isn't limited to motorbikes. The Swedish forest monk Björn Natthiko Lindeblad, in his quietly brilliant book *I May Be Wrong*, shared that his greatest insight from seventeen years of monastic life was that he no longer believed every thought he had.[45] And his preferred meditation? Walking. He found it easier to stay awake, aware, alive, when his body moved. Stillness, again, found within motion.

Let me ask you: Where do you find your stillness?

Maybe it's in cycling. Cooking. Climbing. Surfing. Playing the piano until your fingers blur into the keys. Those moments of being so present in what you're doing that the world can't pull you away.

This chapter is about being aware of and learning to find that rhythm and engage in more of these moments. About letting motion centre you, rather than distract you. Stillness isn't what you're thinking. It's what you *notice*. When you're in motion – but completely in the moment.

Because the world will keep spinning. Your inbox will keep pinging. But amidst all of it, there is a way to ride through with grace. With wonder. With a curiosity and a lust for life.

The Stoic-Zen Fusion

There's a serenity that descends when you're hurtling down a winding road on two wheels, the world blurring into a ribbon of motion and sound. Just the hum of the engine, the lean into each bend, and the subtle conversation between rubber and asphalt. This isn't escapism. It's attention. And paradoxically, it's only when you stop chasing peace that it appears – usually somewhere between third and fourth gear.

Neuroscientists have had a go at explaining this. They talk about the Default Mode Network (DMN), a set of brain regions that light up when you're daydreaming, catastrophising, or mentally replaying that conversation from 2011. But during immersive activities – motorcycling, say, or playing a violin, or watching someone attempt to assemble IKEA furniture without swearing – the DMN quietens down. What's left is presence. Clarity. Sometimes even joy.

At the same time, your brain releases a cocktail of dopamine and norepinephrine. You become alert but calm. Grounded yet responsive. It's a state athletes call "being in the zone," Buddhists call "no-mind," and your average Stoic would just call "Tuesday". Epictetus had no motorcycle – though one suspects he'd have quite enjoyed the austerity of a Triumph Bonneville – but he did have *prosochē*. This was the Stoic discipline of attention. Not the woolly mindfulness peddled in productivity seminars, but something leaner. A readiness of mind. He believed we must remain vigilant to the present, not because it's poetic, but because it's the only place we have any say in how we live.

Marcus Aurelius, writing to himself while dealing with barbarians, floods, and a Senate full of fragile egos, reminded himself daily to return to his "inner citadel".[46] This wasn't retreat in the coward's sense, but a tactical withdrawal into the self. It's not a luxury. It's a survival strategy. Even when Rome is metaphorically – or literally – burning.

And the thing about a motorbike is, it doesn't let you forget this. On roads like Austria's Grossglockner where the corners demand your full respect, there's no room for overthinking. You either pay attention or you end up at the bottom of a mountain debating metaphysics with a red deer. I remember that road – trees casting gold through morning light, corners coiling like questions. And suddenly, without effort or announcement, I wasn't riding the bike. I *was* the bike. No separation. No internal monologue. Just movement. Just being.

The climb began gently. Pine gave way to scrub, then to bare rock, wind-whipped and silvered with frost. The air thinned. The temperature dropped. My breath fogged inside my helmet. Every sense dialled in – the buzz of the engine through my boots, the faint tang of petrol and alpine ice, the steady rhythm of breath and throttle.

Above the treeline, the world opened – vast, stark, silent. No birdsong. No fences. Just switchbacks drawn by the Universe with a ruler and a sense of humour. Time stopped stretching forward or back. It pooled around me, cool and still. There was no destination. Just this. Just now. And then another now. And another. Flow, as Mihaly Csikszentmihalyi coined it, is a state where skill meets challenge in perfect balance.[47] Where action becomes instinct. And where, interestingly, happiness tends to sneak in – not because you were aiming for it, but because you forgot to.

Bruce Lee, whose philosophical punches often landed harder than his physical ones, famously said, "Be like water." Not a call to be passive, but to remain fluid – able to adapt, not snap. Like water, we move best when we stay responsive, adjusting to the shape of life as it comes. This philosophy encourages embracing change and not clinging to rigid patterns or expectations. Seneca said the same, though with fewer high kicks: "Go with the current," he advised. Resistance to what we can't control only creates suffering. Far better to steer with the tide than shout at it.

In martial arts, this mindset becomes a discipline: the art of yielding. Not as weakness, but as a form of intelligent, graceful response. Yielding allows us to deflect with minimal effort, to stay in sympathy with the opposing force. It's not defeat, it's alignment. Like a ballerina pivoting around her partner, both become part of the same movement. No resistance, just flow. And when we ride like that – fully present, fluid – we become the bike, the mountain, the wind. Not fighting the road, but dancing with it.

Björn Natthiko Lindeblad, the Swedish Buddhist monk I mentioned earlier, who later returned to civilian life with more grace than most of us bring to breakfast, practised walking meditation. Step. Breath. Step. Not stopping life, but moving through it deliberately. "Stillness in movement." A nice phrase. And, like most wisdom, completely ordinary when you live it.

So yes – life wobbles. The weather changes. People say one thing and mean another. But you don't have to flinch at every gust. You can train your attention. You can retreat without running away. You can yield – not to give in, but to stop fighting what was never yours to carry. You move with what comes, and suddenly, it has no power over you.

You can ride, walk, work, listen. And now and then, with no fanfare, you'll find the noise drops away. There's no you versus the world. Just the hum of the engine. The curve of the road. And the astonishing fact that – for once – you're here.

Stillness at Speed: The Hidden Gift of Going Fast

On average, phone users tap, swipe, and click around 2,617 times a day – with heavy users interacting with their phones over 5,000 times daily.[48] You might be one of them. Most of us are. It's become a kind of twitch, a digital reflex. It could be a notification that your Amazon parcel's been dispatched. Or that something good might have happened. It probably hasn't. But still, we look. We scroll. We swipe. And then we wonder why we feel so fragmented.

Now imagine a place where you can't do that. Not because you're disciplined or "off-grid," but because to look down might mean hitting a bad line at 80 mph. That's what a motorcycle offers – not escape, exactly, but a forced reckoning. On a bike, your phone stays in your pocket. Not out of virtue. Out of necessity. Survival is the ultimate productivity hack.

The Existential Biker is the name I write, ride, and speak under. It's not a brand or a persona. It's just the most honest version of who I am now: someone who chooses freedom over fear, presence over routine, and experience over expectation.

That wasn't always the case.

Only a few years ago, I was stuck in the loop most people know too well – work, eat, sleep, repeat. A hamster on the wheel. Life had become a checklist. Play was a luxury. Joy was postponed. And somewhere in all that doing, I lost the sense of being.

Then, something shifted.

About seven years ago, I stepped off the treadmill. I stopped trying to be who the world told me I should be. I let go of the script. I let go of the fear that kept me there. And slowly, I started becoming the person I had always sensed I could be – the one who makes her own choices, who feels life rather than simply endures it.

Take Pendine Sands. It's a beach in Wales where the land speed record was once set, and now – on the right day – all manner of vehicles tear across the sand like low-flying aircraft. The start line is oddly peaceful. You're zipped up in leathers. Helmet on. Adrenaline spiking. Yet around you, there's silence.

The kind that exists just before something irreversible happens. It's the eye of the storm.

And then, you go.

There's a strange compression of time. The body moves, but it feels as if thought itself has slowed to a syrupy crawl. One rider described it as *watching himself ride*, as if the mind and body had briefly agreed to stop squabbling and just get on with it. This is presence, pure and sharp. In his essay *De Providentia*, according to Seneca, individuals who are shielded from adversity are denied the chance to cultivate and reveal their moral strength, since virtue becomes visible only when tested by difficulty.[49]

People romanticise Bonneville – and fair enough, with good reason. The salt flats shimmer like something out of myth. But here's the thing: That wasn't the beginning.

The real story started with a wonky eBay purchase – a £1,250 sports bike that barely worked. A beaten and battered 1999-plate Kawasaki Ninja ZX-6R. Stripped wiring. No lights, no indicators, no mirrors. Just a running light, a daytime-only MOT safety certificate with just a couple of months left, and zero pedigree. The poor thing had been thrashed around a track by some lads for the last few years and was destined for the big scrapheap in the sky. Soon. Very soon.

But I figured it only had to get me through one day – just long enough to feel what it was like to ride on sand. A one-ride pony. Or so I thought.

Of course, it wasn't just about the bike. I had no van. No trailer. No idea how to prep a machine for land speed racing. No idea, really, what I was doing at all. And then there was me. I'd never even ridden a sports bike. I was scared of going fast. Scared of corners. Scared of stopping. Scared of . . . well, most of it, really.

But I'd been offered a chance to ride at Bonneville. Bonneville.

Who turns that down?

I had no idea how to prepare. So I called a racing friend for advice – Talan Skeels-Piggins, one of the founders of The Bike Experience, a charity that enables people with disabilities to ride specially adapted bikes. I'd volunteered with the charity a few times and got to know Talan. He's a double 600cc Motorcycle World Champion, so I figured, *He'll know what to do.*

I told him about the opportunity. He paused and said, "Try Pendine. Learn to race on sand first."

"Oh, okay," I said. "When can I pop along?"

"You don't just *pop along*," he said. "There are only two race meets a year – that's when the Ministry of Defence allows racing on what's basically their beach."

"Right. When's the next one?"

A pause.

"In ten days."

I let it sink in. *Ten days.*

I needed a racing licence from the Auto-Cycle Union (ACU) – the national governing body for motorcycle sport in the United Kingdom. I needed to join Straightliners – the club that organises straight-line speed events. I needed an approved helmet, leathers, boots, gloves.

Hell, I needed a *bike*.

I needed to figure out how to get there. And somewhere in the middle of all that, I needed to learn how to actually ride the damn thing.

So I scrambled.

There were phone calls. Paperwork. Gear hunts. Panic-Googling. Late nights on forums. A crash course in race prep. Ten days of chaos. Ten days of questioning what the hell I was doing. Which – as all good stories seem to – culminated in the pub with me perched on the side of a sticky beer-stained table drinking wine and singing very badly.

But the magic? It was in the people.

Yet again, the spirit of the motorcyclist came through.

The night before the race, I met a guy called Stew and the Demon Designs team at The Beach Hotel. Total strangers at the time. They gave me tips and helped me prep the bike – including one thing that probably saved my life: disconnecting the front brake.

On sand, that's the difference between a gentle slide and a high-speed somersault. They helped me calm my nerves. Shared their advice. Shared their marquee. Just solid, generous human beings.

I didn't break any records that weekend. But I did something I never thought I could.

And that changed everything.

Stillness isn't about sitting cross-legged in a candlelit room trying to manifest calm. It's about full presence. Clarity under pressure.

"Stillness is not about inactivity. It's about being steady while the world spins around you," wrote Ryan Holiday in *Stillness Is the Key*.

He's right. Most of our paralysis lives in the anticipation. Once you're doing the thing – on the sand, gripping the throttle – there's no room left for fear. There's only the next moment.

Later, I went over 200 mph at Elvington, a former RAF airfield runway in North Yorkshire. On tarmac. On a borrowed bike, lent to me on the spur of the moment by the iconic racer Jack Frost. No insurance. No big plan. I was just there. Asking questions. Saying yes when someone said, "Want to have a go?"

I'll never forget that run. The moment I crossed the light markers, something happened that I still can't quite explain.

It was as if time paused – not slowed, but truly paused. Everything dropped away. There was no before or after, just a single, vivid now. I wasn't thinking. I wasn't even riding, not really. I was *in* it – completely present, completely still, despite the speed.

I remember it in sharp detail. The exact blue of the sky. The feel of the tarmac. And there, at the far end of the runway, a Vulcan bomber – massive, otherworldly, like a silent witness. I was at once aware of the very small, and the very large. My part in the cosmos was suddenly *all* of it.

It felt like the world had opened up, just for a second, and let me see everything at once.

It wasn't quiet – but it was still. Stillness doesn't always mean silence. Sometimes it's found in the roar, the rush, the total surrender to the moment. And when it finds you like that – it stays with you.

This is what Stoicism taught me. Not how to detach from life, but how to *live* it more fully. Stillness is not withdrawal. It's alignment. Marcus Aurelius spoke of keeping the mind "untangled" and "upright".[50] That's what riding gave me: a clear line through the noise.

But let's be honest – not everyone can take off on a motorbike, jump on a boat or escape for months in a campervan. Some have debts, children, routines that feel immovable. We can't blow up our life. And I get that.

Still – we can find your own Pendine or Elvington in smaller ways. These moments of stillness add up. They build a sense of self not tied to roles or outcomes. They reconnect you with the one thing your phone can't give you: presence.

And if you *can* make a big change – do it. Don't wait. Don't let comfort con you into staying put or let yourself be held down by the trappings of the lifestyle that costs so much to maintain you are still tethered to working in a job you don't enjoy. If there's an ache in your heart, go. Take the cruise. Ride the bike. Write the book. Or buy a scrappy, tired, battle-worn bike off eBay and see what happens. Just say yes.

Because if you don't, someone else will end up telling the story of your life – and they'll only know the edited version.

Better you live it fully, and tell it in your own words. You don't need to quit your job, grow a beard, or move to Bhutan. But you do need to ask the hard questions:

What am I distracting myself from? What am I postponing?

For many, the answer is change.

I get it. I worked in the corporate world for decades – doing okay for myself on the outside, but quietly shrinking inside. I carried a deep yearning to change, to experience this glorious world more fully, and yet I was too afraid to take off the familiar identity of mother, white-collar worker, dependable grown-up. It was comfortable. But it wasn't alive.

That version of me – well-dressed, well-behaved, always on time – was keeping me from the pull of something deeper. The yearnings of my essential self. The person I was born to be before the world told me who I ought to be.

Most of us don't fear death as much as we fear the death of identity – the moment we admit that who we are no longer fits who we're becoming. And yet, change is the only real certainty.

As Rumi wrote, "You were born with wings, why prefer to crawl through life?"

So start small.

You don't need a beach. You don't need a new job. But you do need to say yes to the part of you that's been quietly tapping your shoulder, asking if this – this loop, this role, this rush – is really it.

Because if not now, when?

Cultivating Stillness in Motion

There is something quietly revolutionary in learning how to *pause* without stopping. Not just physically, but inwardly. To be still – not like a statue, but like a mountain in the wind. Most of us spend our days reacting: to emails, to headlines, to the sound of someone chewing too loudly two desks over. We flinch from moment to moment, constantly interrupted by the urgent but rarely by the essential.

The Stoics, suspicious of drama, knew this inner flinching was the real threat. Stillness, for them, wasn't the absence of movement – it was mastery within it. A readiness. A lack of wasted energy.

As one Zen saying puts it: "You should sit in meditation for twenty minutes a day – unless you're too busy. Then you should sit for an hour."

Stillness isn't just about silence. It's about clarity. Attention. Choosing to be fully where you are, especially when everything pulls you elsewhere. You don't need incense. Just a pulse you can feel and a moment you don't squander.

Because if you can't be still in the chaos, you'll never be still at all.

Decision-making thrives on this kind of poise. When the mind is noisy, it seizes on whatever offers closure – confirmation bias, impulse, someone else's opinion dressed up as certainty. But when you create space inside yourself, you're less likely to mistake panic for urgency. Stillness allows the deeper mind to speak – the one that isn't just trying to win the argument or clear the inbox.

There's a practical rhythm to this, especially if you happen to ride motorcycles. One technique that's served me well is what I've come to call "breath-throttle sync". Inhale on the straights, exhale through the bends. It sounds simple, and it is. But that's the point. The breath becomes a metronome, anchoring the body and keeping the panic-prone part of the brain too busy to catastrophise. Exhaling into a curve slows the heart rate just enough to keep you from tensing the wrong muscle at the wrong moment.

Then there's the "peripheral vision drill". Most new riders focus too hard on the centre of the road, especially when scared. This narrows the visual field, creating tunnel vision – both literal and psychological. But softening your gaze, letting your eyes take in the wider frame, has an oddly calming effect. It reminds the nervous system that it's not under attack. It also reminds you, rather usefully, that the road is wide and you are not, in fact, heading straight for that hedge.

And for those without a motorbike in the garage? Stillness doesn't require leather or petrol.

Try walking like Lindeblad. Not power-walking, or stomping to the station while texting. Just walking. One foot, then the next. Noticing how your foot meets the ground like a gear clicking into place.

Or find "micro-flow" moments. Washing dishes, brushing your teeth, folding laundry. The modern mind wants to outsource or rush these things, but that's precisely why they matter. Slow them down – not because someone told you to, but because presence has value, even when no one's watching.

Robert Pirsig wrote in *Zen and the Art of Motorcycle Maintenance* that quality isn't a thing – it's an event.[51] A relationship. The space between you and what you're doing when you're actually doing it. Not multi-tasking. Not waiting for it to be over. But paying attention. That's what the Stoics were getting at. And the Buddhists. And the mechanics who actually enjoy their work.

So, no, the world won't slow down for you. But you can cultivate a kind of stillness in motion – a calm eye in a fast-moving frame. And when you do, decisions come cleaner. Focus sharpens. And every now and then, you remember what it feels like to be fully human – not driven, but driving.

Chapter 6

Riding with the World

"Look deep into nature, and then you will understand everything better."
— Albert Einstein

MOTORCYCLISTS LIVE IN THE elements, not behind glass. They smell the world, feel its breath. The average driver, sealed inside their box of glass and steel, might tell you they "drove through" the Alps or "did" the Highlands, but on a bike, there is no such illusion.

You can't scroll your phone while threading through a mountain pass. You are there. Exposed. Honest. You ride not *through* the world, but *with* it.

There's a pass in the Pyrenees I think about often. No name worth remembering – just a long stretch of winding asphalt where the trees fall away and the sky takes over. I cut the engine near the summit once, just to hear the quiet. No traffic. No birdsong. Just the cooling ping of metal and the faint crack of a hawk's cry carried on wind. The air was sharp and pine-fresh. And for a few long moments, I simply stood there, breathing. No phone, no podcast, no point to be made. Just breath. Just presence.

The Stoics would have called this *sympatheia* – a felt sense that all things are interconnected. That you are not outside nature, but of it. Not an observer, but a participant. "All things are intertwined with one another, a sacred bond unites them . . . for they have been arranged together in their places and make up the same ordered universe."[52]

It's an idea that's both comforting and terrifying. Comforting, because it means we're not alone. Terrifying, because it means we can't pretend to be. Every decision, every action, echoes. Riding makes that clear. You accelerate into the wind, and it pushes back. You ride through rain, and it gets inside your gloves, down your neck. The world answers. It always does.

The modern world does its best to insulate us from this fact. Cruise control, heated seats, predictive navigation – clever stuff, to be sure, but it also dulls the edges of real life. We're turning down the volume on the very thing we're part of. Henry David Thoreau warned of this in *Walden* when he said, "Our inventions are wont to be pretty toys, which distract our attention from serious things."[53] The world becomes a backdrop. We forget that it's alive. That we're in it. When you remove the windscreen, both literally and metaphorically, something shifts. The frame of separation disappears. You're no longer just seeing. You're participating.

But let's not get too misty-eyed. Riding through nature isn't always transcendent. Sometimes it's frustrating, exhausting, or just very, very wet. There was one ride early in my return to motorcycling – down to Sennen Cove in Cornwall. I'd joined a group called Explorer's Connect, run by my friend Belinda Kirk – an extraordinary woman who's brought adventure into the lives of so many through shared experiences. I was heading to a weekend of water sports, including paddleboarding and swimming with seals.

Little did I know I'd encounter a level of wetness on the A30 that rivalled actual deep diving – long before I ever reached the sea.

It rained so hard that at one point I started laughing out loud, not because it was funny, but because resisting it had become pointless. There's a kind of liberation in that, too. Nature doesn't care how you feel. It just exists. The moment you stop fighting it, you start experiencing it. When I was within three miles of Sennen I actually slowed down, so I could savour the last few moments of this extreme-weather ride.

Josh Waitzkin – chess prodigy, Jiu Jitsu black belt, and author of *The Art of Learning* – once noticed how often parents would say, "The weather's bad – it's raining – we can't go outside."[54] When his son was born, he decided to flip that script. Every type of weather became an invitation to explore. No control, just curiosity. He and his son Jack haven't skipped a single storm. Rain, snow – it's always the right time to step outside and play.

A 2019 University of Michigan study found that twenty to thirty minutes in nature drops cortisol levels 21.3% per hour.[55] Another from UCSF linked "awe walks" to improved emotional well-being.[56] These researchers could've saved time by asking any motorcyclist: Yes, the world does help you feel better when you stop trying to control it.

Of course, not every ride is a meditation. Some are cold, chaotic, and smell strongly of livestock. But even those rides remind you of something simple: You're alive. You're moving. You're not just watching the world – you're breathing it.

That's where we're headed in this chapter. To explore the kind of riding – and living – that doesn't resist the world, but listens to it.

How often do you tell yourself the conditions aren't right?

What if nature isn't an option, but a relationship?

Stoic *Sympatheia* in Motion

There's a particular kind of silence that falls when you kill the engine at the top of a pass. It's not the silence of absence, but the silence of everything falling into place. The wind doesn't so much howl as it listens with you. The land, the sky, the machine – they all stop pretending to be separate. That's the moment, I think, when you stop riding through the world and start riding with it.

Sympatheia is one of those terms that sounds faintly like a condition until you realise it's the condition you've been hoping for all along. Marcus Aurelius described it as the interdependence of all things – a sacred bond, not sentimental, but structural. You don't make it happen.[57] You notice that it's already true.

To ride with *sympatheia* is to understand that you're not the main character in the story. You're a line in a shared paragraph. Not conformity as compliance. But as alignment. Like a wheel that spins true.

Robert Pirsig captured this in *Zen and the Art of Motorcycle Maintenance*. "On a cycle the frame is gone . . . you're in the scene, not just watching it anymore."[58] It's not metaphorical. It's literal. You are in the wind. You are in the rain. You are undeniably here.

And that, for me, is the metaphor that keeps unfolding. Motorcycling strips away the filters. The wind is wind. The rain is rain. There's no temperature control, no curated playlist, no algorithmic newsfeed designed to match your mood. There is only what's happening – and your response to it.

The Stoics would approve. Their goal was never to remove discomfort. It was to meet life unshielded, with discernment and courage. Seneca wrote that true happiness comes not from escaping hardship, but from developing the internal condition to meet it.[59] Riding offers no escape. It offers confrontation. And that confrontation, strangely, becomes communion.

I remember a ride across the Yorkshire Dales where the road wound through hills like a half-remembered dream – sharp turns, blind crests, cambers that tilted the wrong way. For a while I fought it, trying to ride the landscape as I wanted it to be – straight, clean, predictable. But the road didn't care about my preferences. It just *was*. So I stopped wrestling it. I let the bike move with the contours, not against them. I matched my line to the lay of the land. That's when the ride changed. It became not easier, but smoother. Not safer, but more connected.

That's what Stoicism teaches. Not detachment, but attention. Not arm's-length analysis, but full-bodied participation. You don't transcend the world. You drop into it. Fully. And in doing so, something surprising happens: You stop feeling like a separate thing trying to navigate nature, and you start to recognise yourself as part of it.

Sympatheia isn't about feeling fuzzy. It's about reality. The shared one. The one that includes tractor drivers, midges, traffic jams, hawks, and the odd person who lets you pass with a nod. You're not above it. You're not beneath it. You're simply with it.

So ride – or walk, or stand still if you must – but let the world in. Let it remind you that presence is not a performance. It's a kind of honesty. And it begins when you stop filtering the world and start feeling it.

Riding the Current

You don't fight the wind on a motorbike. You lean into it. Try to resist, and it throws you off balance. Accept its push, and something strange happens – you glide. Riding becomes less of a struggle, more of a dance. That's when it hits you: Maybe life is like this too.

The Stoics thought so. Epictetus said the goal is to "keep your moral purpose in a state of conformity with nature."[60] It sounds austere, like something barked by a monk in sandals. What he meant was aligning yourself with the actual shape of things. With what is. With reality. Most of our suffering, he argued, comes not from life itself, but from the way we try to bend it to our will, like a man trying to stop a river with a broom.

I've done that, of course. We all have. When a plan unravels, or someone lets us down, or the weather ignores the forecast, the temptation is to grip harder.

Fix. Solve. Control. But I've learned more from things going sideways than from smooth, forgettable rides.

Take the time I collected my nearly-new Indian Scout in Gloucester – the bike model I'd fallen head over heels for during my sprint through Death Valley. I bought it without a second thought about how it might handle British roads, let alone mini-roundabouts in Surrey. I turned up with none of the right gear, just the giveaway Eaglerider leather jacket from the US trip and some old riding trousers with worn-out Harley Davidson boots. I was woefully unprepared for the 150-mile journey home. And by the time I set off, it was already getting dark. And cold. I rode for an hour, freezing. When I could no longer feel my fingers, I pulled over to warm my hands on the exhaust. They were stained blue from the dye in my cheap leather gloves.

That's when it hit me. I was doomed.

No plan. No backup. No way to keep going. So I did the only sensible thing: I rang Justin, my daughter's partner, for help. I took refuge in a Harvester. Walked in like a drowned rat. All eyes were on me. I sat alone, starving, with only a bottle of ketchup for company. I thought I'd looked so cool, roaring off into the dusk. But now here I was, soggy, defeated – and laughing. Not at the situation. At myself. At the absurdity of trying to out-muscle the world.

That soggy evening in the Harvester wasn't the ride I'd imagined. But it was the one I was given. And maybe that's the point. Life doesn't hand out perfect plans – it offers us moments. And it's up to us to meet them, not mold them

That night, I wasn't just a cold, wet woman on a bike. I was part of something larger: a quiet choreography of road, weather, mishap, and human kindness. A misadventure, yes – but also a moment of belonging. To place. To people. To the pulse of something shared and wild. I'd tried to muscle through nature, but nature was never the enemy. It was the teacher.

And somehow, that felt right.

Pirsig gets this too. "In a car you're always in a compartment, and because you're used to it you don't realise that through the car windscreen everything is just more TV. You're a passive observer and it is all moving by you boringly in a frame. On a cycle the frame is gone. You're completely in contact with it all. You're in the scene, not just watching it anymore, and the sense of presence is overwhelming. That concrete whizzing by five inches below your feet is the real thing."[61]

But it's more than presence. It's participation.

You're not simply on the road – you are the road, moving through space with the sky above, the tyres below, the hillside exhaling beside you. You're stitched into it, muscle and machine and moment. *Sympatheia* isn't a lofty ideal – it's your hands on the bars, your breath matching the wind, your fate braided into the world's without resistance.

That concrete five inches below? That's not the edge of danger. That's the place where your life and the world's life meet. Where the membrane thins, and for just a moment, you remember you're not separate after all.

Nature, the Stoics argue, has its own rhythm. It doesn't consult your spreadsheet. It doesn't issue warnings. The clouds will rain whether you brought waterproofs or not. What Stoicism offers is a kind of moral aikido – stop trying to overpower the moment and start flowing with it.

There's a practice I've started doing when things go wrong on the road. Flat tyre, wrong turn, closed café. Instead of reacting, I pause and ask: "What's the current here? Where is it already flowing?" Often it's not where I wanted to go. But, almost always, it's where I needed to be.

This isn't about giving up. It's about giving in – strategically. Life has its own intelligence. What looks like failure is often redirection. What feels like delay might be an invitation. A conversation at a layby. A view you wouldn't have stopped for. A kindness from a stranger who shouldn't have even been there.

To align with nature, in the Stoic sense, is not to drift aimlessly, but to paddle with the river, not against it. It's active trust. Not that things will go your way, but that you will find your way, through them.

So the next time the wind rises, don't stiffen. Lean. The road knows what it's doing. And if you stop seeing it as an obstacle, you might just find yourself somewhere better than planned.

The World as Co-Rider

Many times on the bike, I've felt like a bird on the wing. The kind that glides rather than flaps – buoyed by something invisible but entirely real. The air on my cheeks, the scent of sage or diesel or freshly turned soil, the sun slipping across my shoulders like a companion rather than a concept. Riding does that. It puts you in the world, not on it. You're not behind a screen or wrapped in steel and silence. You're porous. Open. Part of the scene rather than sealed off from it.

I've ridden through Moroccan deserts in the morning and been face to face with snowcaps by teatime. I've watched lush hills become bone-dry dust within a few miles, as if someone quietly adjusted the colour palette. I've waved to farmers turning hay, nuns tending gardens, small boys with sticks pretending to joust, all of us nodding across the gulf of difference with the same unspoken phrase: *Isn't it something, this day?*

It's in these moments – fleeting, unpolished, alive – that the Stoics whisper their old truth: You are not apart from the world. You are of it. Not metaphorically, but literally.

As the astrophysicist and science communicator Carl Sagan famously wrote, "The nitrogen in our DNA, the calcium in our teeth, the iron in our blood, the carbon in our apple pies were made in the interiors of collapsing stars. We are made of starstuff." That's not poetic indulgence. It's astrophysics. A reminder that the boundary between us and everything else is far more porous than we like to believe. We belong here. We are built of the same matter as the sky.

You, me, tortoises, telegraph poles.

Ah yes – the tortoise.

We were riding along in Morocco, the kind of scorching plain that makes you think of spaghetti Westerns and how little water you've packed. I was sweep, bringing up the rear, while our lead guide, Billy, wound down a windy road and pulled up sharp. Kickstand down. No explanation. He just got off and started walking. For a moment I thought, Well, if he's going for a pee, that's a dramatic choice of venue.

But then I saw it – a tortoise. About the size of a large teacup. Just shuffling across the path, as if it had all the time in the world and wasn't remotely troubled by the combined rumble of 10,000ccs of European machinery humming in the sun. Without a word, Billy knelt down, scooped the creature up with both hands, and gently carried it to safety.

There was a quiet that settled over us then. Not the usual engine-off stillness, but something else. Reverence, maybe. Or recognition. In that moment, a dozen humans and a dozen machines bowed – literally and figuratively – to one ounce of blind, shelled life.

That's *sympatheia* in action. Seeing yourself in the "other". Realising that your momentum isn't more important than someone else's existence. Even if that someone has four legs and a dome for a roof.

Riding exposes you to this again and again. A thunderstorm rolls in and soaks you to the skin. You're not annoyed – you laugh. One friend described me in those moments as like "a mad woman throwing shit". He wasn't wrong. But that madness is its own kind of sanity. When you stop fighting the elements and let them baptise you, what follows isn't irritation – it's joy. Because you've stopped measuring the day by comfort and started measuring it by presence.

And here's the thing: Science backs this up. Time in nature, even a brief exposure, reduces cortisol levels, restores attention, and boosts emotional resilience.[62] The body knows what the Stoics tried to teach: You were built for this world – not for filtered air and scrolling thumbs, but for wind, mud, and awe.

Gratitude arrives unbidden when you're too wet to check your phone.

So the next time you ride – or walk, or simply open a window – ask yourself not what you can get from the world, but what you might give it. Attention. Care. Reverence. A hand to a tortoise, a wave to a farmer, a laugh in the rain.

You're not travelling through the world. You are travelling *with* it.

Trusting the Rhythm

There's a moment on every long ride when you stop trying to make good time and start letting time make something good of you.

You ease off the throttle. You stop scanning for the next petrol station or the weather app or the number of miles remaining. Instead, you let the day unfold. The sun arcs overhead like it always does. The shadows lengthen. You catch yourself noticing the colour of the wheat or the way a bird cuts sideways across the sky. You start to suspect that the world might just know what it's doing – and your job isn't to fight it but to ride alongside.

There's a kind of peace in that. A sanity. But it runs against the grain of modern life, where agency is king and surrender is confused with weakness. We're told to "make it happen", "push through", "manifest your destiny" – as though the world were some fussy old horse you can force into a gallop if only you kick hard enough.

But what if the wiser move is to listen for the rhythm beneath the noise? To trust that sometimes the road is long because it needs to be?

In Seneca's essay *De Vita Beata*, he notes that a wise person is at peace with what they have, regardless of their circumstances.[63] Not because he lacks ambition, but because he understands the limits of control. The world spins. Winds change. Other people say no. The job falls through. The rain doesn't stop. You can't brute-force serenity.

So how do you live with that?

Start by asking: What's mine to carry? Your choices, your responses, your values. And then ask: What's not? The traffic. The weather. The past. Other people's egos. Then take a breath, unclench your grip, and go forward with fewer expectations but more attention.

Practical? Absolutely. Next time your plans fall apart – try not planning the next ones quite so tightly. Next time the motorway slows to a crawl – turn off the podcast and listen to the silence. There's music in it. And next time you're tempted to force something to happen – pause. Ask whether it's really your job to pull the river upstream.

Trust, the Stoics teach us, is not naïveté. It's courage. The courage to ride with life, not against it. To work with the grain, not sand it down. You are not just an agent of change, you are also a participant in a pattern larger than you can fully see.

And when you ride with that awareness – something shifts. You stop feeling behind. You stop trying to win. You start noticing. Maybe even smiling.

That's not resignation. That's wisdom with a kick-start.

PART THREE

DIRECTION

You make the call. Every turn, every stop, every refusal to follow the crowd.

Direction comes from tuning in, not speeding up. You listen — to your body, to the people who matter, to the work that holds weight. These chapters follow that thread. The one that keeps tugging at you when you're off course. It's always there, waiting for you to notice.

Chapter 7

Where You Look Is Where You Go

"The soul becomes dyed with the colour of its thoughts."
— Marcus Aurelius

Your mind is a paranoid storyteller, spinning worst-case scenarios with the desperate creativity of a drunk facing last call. Evolution wired it this way – predictable pain always felt safer than chaos. Two million years ago, this instinct kept you alive. *Where's dinner? Am I dinner?* Simple questions with immediate stakes. But today? That same survival mechanism just makes you crash your damn bike.

I learned this the hard way on the Grossglockner, Austria's highest pass, where the guardrails are as thin as a bureaucrat's patience. One moment, I'm leaned into a hairpin, the bike humming beneath me. The next, my eyes lock onto the sheer drop like a moth hypnotised by a lightbulb. *Don't go over. Don't go over.* My tyres, obedient as ever, followed the unspoken command – straight toward the edge.

The world narrowed to sparks flying from grinding metal, the shriek of footpegs against steel, and my own heartbeat roaring in my ears louder than the engine. For one suspended second, physics held its breath. Then – grip. The bike corrected. I'd escaped becoming a cautionary tale, but the lesson stuck: I hadn't almost died because of the curve. I'd almost died because I'd *stared at death instead of the road.*

Riders call this *target fixation.* Focus too long on the tree mid-corner, and you'll veer into it. Obsess over the pothole, and you'll hit it dead-centre. It's not a metaphor. It's Newtonian law – your body follows your gaze as reliably as a bike follows its rider's input. Handlebar or hypothalamus, the principle doesn't change.

Yet the solution isn't *positive thinking.* Platitudes won't save you when you're sliding toward gravel. What works is *rewiring your gaze* – training your focus like a muscle, until the right line becomes instinct. And sometimes, you can't do it alone. Just as a rider needs a coach to spot bad habits, we all need that outside voice once in a while to create that sudden flick of mental handlebars and jolt us toward a new sightline.

The Body Knows Before You Do

Life doesn't always shift gears politely. Sometimes it kicks you in the teeth mid-sentence.

I found this out when a colleague I was giving a lift to interrupted one of my usual meaning-of-life tangents – I was off on one about the block theory of time or something – when he turned to me with, "What on earth are you doing working at Maritime Publishing?"

I blinked.

"What?"

He repeated it, slower this time.

"Every time we talk, it's philosophy, psychology, or some mind-bending science. You just don't seem to belong here."

He was right. I'd been ignoring the signs: the Sunday night dread, the way my shoulders curled forward at my desk like I was serving a sentence. The clenched jaw. The stiff neck. That "mild ache" I blamed on aging? That was my skeleton begging me to move. Your body talks in code long before your mind's ready to listen.

That single comment – offhand, but honest – sparked the slow process of waking up to myself. I don't remember the rest of the drive, but I remember how that sentence hit: like a steel-toe boot to the soul.

My perspective shifted. And when perspective shifts, reality starts to remap.

On a motorcycle, truth isn't up for debate. You stay upright or you don't. Physics doesn't offer participation trophies. There are no corporate retreats for gravity. It's just you, the machine, and whatever thoughts you're entertaining when traction disappears.

I saw it happen on the A4069. Sarah, a new rider, was doing fine – until she saw the pothole. Her body locked on like a missile.

"I knew I shouldn't look," she said afterward, gloves pressed to her hips. "But I couldn't look away."

Target fixation. We all do it. Sarah stared at the pothole. I'd been staring at promotions, praise, and approval.

There was a stretch – after the promotions but before the panic attacks – when I tried to steer life by other people's opinions. Every meeting became a performance. Every email felt like a tightrope walk over imagined judgment. Like Sarah, I knew it wasn't working. But looking away from validation felt like staring into the abyss.

Until my doctor, in a drab NHS office flanked by motivational posters on handwashing, looked at me and said I was on course for a breakdown. He might as well have said I was target-fixating on my own destruction.

Your brain doesn't respond well to negative commands. Tell yourself, "Don't crash," and it fixates on crashing. Daniel Wegner proved this with his white bear experiment: The more you try not to think of one, the more it dominates your mind.

This is the brain's ironic process at work. To avoid something, you first have to picture it. That's how it takes over.

The fix? Positive direction.

Swap avoidance for action.

Not "Don't fall," but "Stay balanced."

Not "Don't panic," but "Breathe steady."

As Martha Beck puts it, the body has its own vocabulary – tightness, ease, expansion, resistance – and physical cues like relaxed shoulders or deeper breathing often tell us before our minds do that something is aligned. She refers to this as our internal compass, guiding us toward our "True North" and away from dissonance. The real challenge isn't recognising the signal – it's learning to listen.[64]

Your values show up there too: in the gut punch of wrongness when you betray them, in the expansive breath when you align. The experiences that shook you – both glorious and terrible – are compass points written in the body's language. That time you cried at a stranger's kindness. The job that made your hands shake before every meeting. The moment on the bike when everything clicked. These aren't just memories – they're your Rosetta Stone.

The mind follows the images you feed it. So give it better ones.

The night before my Bonneville run, I didn't lie awake fearing the salt flats. I rode them in my head. Over and over. I pictured the light on the surface, the bars in my hands, the blur of mile markers as I hit full throttle. I ran the whole course mentally until it felt like muscle memory.

On race day, I knelt in the salt, closed my eyes, and did it again – start to finish. I even timed it. So when I finally swung my leg over the bike, it wasn't my first run anymore.

When my doctor once said, "Find your line," I thought he was being metaphorical. Now I know it was the only kind of instruction the brain truly understands: something to move toward.

The road teaches you without mercy: You don't overcome obstacles by fighting them. You look past them. Not with hope, but with precision.

That's the essence of this chapter.

Not positive thinking. Not blind optimism. Just refocusing.

Knowing what matters. Finding your line. And trusting yourself to follow it.

Happiness isn't the goal – it's what shows up when you're pointed in the right direction.

The Man with the Machete

Focus on fear, and you shape yourself around it. Focus on what matters – courage, clarity, purpose – and your life begins to lean, inch by inch, in that direction. The ancients called this *prosochē*: the discipline of attention. Not productivity hacks. Not forced positivity. Just noticing – *What are you feeding your mind? Where does your gaze keep landing without you realising?*

Take my boiler obsession. For weeks, I was convinced it was dying. Every gurgle sounded like a death rattle. Every lukewarm shower? Proof. When the engineer finally came, he found nothing wrong. The boiler was fine. *I* was the problem – I'd trained my brain to hunt for disaster, and like a loyal hound, it brought me exactly what I'd asked for.

We do this everywhere. In relationships. At work. With ourselves. We fixate on flaws, brace for failure, rehearse disappointment – *and call it being realistic.* But fear isn't foresight. It's a script we write before the curtain rises.

I learned this the hard way in a Malaysian rainforest, where a machete taught me the cost of seeing what isn't there.

The air hung thick as wet wool. My shirt clung to my back like a second skin as I pushed deeper into the jungle, flip-flops slipping on damp leaves. Monkey Beach lay deserted – just a few listing umbrellas, a stall selling warm Fanta, and me, the idiot tourist wandering off-trail.

Then I heard it: the *crack* of a branch. The lazy *swish* of steel.

I turned. Fifty feet back, a young man followed. Frayed shirt. Flip-flops. A machete swinging at his side like a pendulum.

This is how foreigners become cautionary tales. My gut turned to ice. I measured distances – the boat, the trees, the brutal truth that flip-flops aren't made for sprinting. I could already see the consulate report: *Overconfident Brit found with adventurous spirit, missing head.*

So I did what any reasonable person would do: I turned *toward* him, grinned like a madman, and pointed at the blade, "What's that for?"

He stared. Then made a sinuous motion with his hand. "Snakes."

Turns out, he wasn't a threat. He was a *guardian*. The machete? Jungle maintenance. The "stalking"? Him keeping pace in case I stumbled into a king cobra. He even offered me water.

But I'd seen none of that. Why? Because fear had already written the script: *Danger. Run. Die.* I'd missed his smile, his easy posture, the bottle in his hand – all because my brain was too busy screening its own horror movie.

Here's the alternative: Shift from fear to focus. Even though your brain can't unsee danger, it can choose a better focal point. When you catch yourself spiralling:

Swap *"Don't screw this up"* → *"Stay present, stay clear."*

Trade *"Don't panic"* → *"Breathe deep, feet grounded."*

Give your mind somewhere worth going, and it will steer there. Usually. *(Exception: If an actual machete-wielding man is chasing you? Run first. Philosophise later.)*

Where you look *is* where you go – so aim somewhere worth heading.

How Thoughts Shape Reality

The shadows were stretching long when Steve and I pushed my Yamaha TTR250 across the road into the woods. Technically, we weren't supposed to ride in there, but someone had built a makeshift mini-course – probably for mountain bikes – with twists and humps too tempting to ignore. It was quiet, out of the way, and we figured: What's the harm in a quick play?

That bike – my faithful TTR – had always stirred something in me. A reliable little workhorse, it was similar to the one Lois Pryce rode across Iran in *Revolutionary Ride*. Her book had blown something wide open. With humour, grit, and open-hearted curiosity, she gave voice to the real Iran – not the headlines, but the human stories. Her encounters with warmth, poetry, and radical kindness made me ache for adventure. I wasn't in Iran. I was in a damp wood. But still . . . something was brewing.

Off-road riding has never been my strength. I tense up. I see a rut and immediately picture myself in it. It's not fear, exactly – it's a kind of habitual defeat.

I wish I were better, but I know there's no shortcut to skill. You have to practice.

Steve, on the other hand, was pure grace. Agile, precise, absurdly confident. Watching him ride my TTR was like watching a squirrel on a caffeine high – quick, nimble, and maddeningly fearless.

Then he handed the bike to me.

"Your turn."

Fine, I said. But not doing that bit. Or that one. Especially not that ridiculous mound that looked like it had been stolen from a ski slope. "I'll just stick to this loop."

But Steve wouldn't have it.

"You can do this," he said.

"No, I really can't."

"You absolutely have the skill."

"Absolutely do not."

I was about to tell him – genuinely – to piss off. This wasn't funny anymore. And then I saw his face. He wasn't joking. His eyes were lit with something fierce and sincere. He meant it. He believed in me.

And in that second, everything went quiet – the wind, the birds, even my excuses.

Something shifted.

Can I do it?

I can do it.

I will do it.

Suddenly, I was every action hero from my childhood: Steve McQueen, Clint Eastwood, Chuck Norris. (Clearly, the women's movement hadn't reached '70s action TV when I was a kid.) I pulled my visor down.

This was it. My moment.

Fuck it. I rode.

And I nearly made it. Nearly. I got halfway up the tall mound, then fell backward and sideways, sliding down like a slow-motion comedy sketch. But I knew now. I could *do* it.

I got up, dusted myself off, got back on, leaned forward, throttled harder – and this time, I flew. Right to the top. And on the way down, I threw in a little jump. Just because I could.

It turns out, the hillock didn't change. I did.

What had looked like a wall was just a bump in the path.

And it all started with a single look from someone who believed in me.

My reality shifted the moment my perception did. And from then on, I never saw obstacles quite the same way again.

Awareness is the master key. You can't change what you don't notice, and you'll never steer true while staring at the gravel. Your brain makes no distinction between real and imagined threats. Picture being chased by a lion, and your body responds instantly

– adrenaline floods, heart pounds, muscles tense for flight. This survival mechanism once saved lives. Today, it makes your palms sweat over an angry email.

Picture losing your job. Or being humiliated in front of people you admire. Or dropping your bike in front of a row of Harley riders you were hoping to impress. Your brain reacts on cue: adrenaline, cortisol, tight chest, sweaty palms. Fight-or-flight kicks in – without the fight or the flight. The threat doesn't need to be real. It just has to feel real. And your imagination, uninvited, is often convincing.

Even a memory of someone we love – or have lost – can leave us feeling punch-drunk or hollow. That ache in the chest? A real thing, courtesy of cortisol or oxytocin, depending on whether it's a longing or a heartbreak. Your thoughts – your focus – change your biochemistry.

The Stoics would've been fascinated by modern neuroscience. They believed attention is a choice – not always an easy one, granted, but still yours to make. The *discipline of assent*, as Epictetus called it, is the practice of examining each thought as it arrives. "Is this true? Is this helpful? Am I staring at the edge of the cliff again?" What they called *assent* – the moment you either let a thought take root or let it pass – lines up closely with what psychologists now call *appraisal*. Epictetus put it plainly: "We are disturbed not by things, but by the opinions we form about them."[65]

And your body, as it turns out, tends to agree. And yet, with all this potential for mischief, imagination can also be a tool. In 2004, a group of people were asked to imagine lifting weights – no gym, no dumbbells, just focused thought. A few weeks later, their strength had increased by over 13.5%. Not because they'd done any physical reps, but because their brains had. Their brains activated motor pathways as if they were training for real. The muscles stayed still, but the nervous system adapted anyway.[66]

Guided meditation often asks you to picture a forest or a shoreline. Not because you'll magically end up in Cornwall, but because your brain doesn't need to be there to feel there. Breathing slows. Blood pressure drops. Your parasympathetic system, the one responsible for "rest and digest," finally gets a word in.

The Reticular Activating System (RAS) is a strange bit of brainstem circuitry involved in regulating wakefulness and attention. It acts a bit like a mental gatekeeper: Tell it what matters, and it begins tuning your awareness toward anything that aligns.[67] Set a goal – "I want to lead motorcycle tours in the Alps" – and it starts letting in the relevant people, conversations, and opportunities. Suddenly, you notice routes, gear ads, and conversations with friends of friends. It's not the universe handing you breadcrumbs. It's your focus that's waking up. You start seeing what was always there, filtered through a new lens.

It sounds simple. Almost insultingly so. But as any rider knows, it's also everything. You don't fight the road. You don't outmuscle a tight bend. You choose your line, focus your vision, and the bike follows. Not because of willpower, but because of alignment. Sight. Intention. Flow.

In modern day, that principle, oddly enough, doesn't just apply to the tarmac. It rides with you through the rest of your life. The Stoics understood this long before helmets and full-body leathers were a thing. Epictetus wrote, "The chief task in life is simply this: to identify and separate matters so that I can say clearly to myself which are externals not under my control, and which have to do with the choices I actually control."[68] What he was really getting at is attention. Noticing where your mind is pointing, and steering it back when it veers off.

The practice isn't perfection – it's persistence. Not eliminating distractions, but catching them quicker. Not white-knuckle willpower, but the gentle nudge of realigned attention. So clean your mental visor often. When in doubt, ask:

Where am I looking now?

Then point your gaze – and your life – somewhere worth going.

The Direction of Attention

In that split second before the turn — before the wrong words leave your mouth, before fear freezes your muscles — you still have a choice. Stare at the loose gravel, the mistake, the disaster you're trying to avoid, and sure enough, that's where you'll end up. Or lift your gaze to where the road still holds possibility.

It sounds deceptively simple. But as any rider knows, this is everything. You don't conquer corners through brute force. You don't argue with physics. You choose your line, fix your vision, and let the bike follow. Not through willpower, but alignment. Sight. Intention. Flow.

I learned this the hard way — on bikes, in bars, in the long stretch of nights when the writing process mocked me. You don't write by obsessing over bad sentences. You write the next word, and then the next. You don't stay sober by thinking, *Don't drink*. You drink coffee, walk the dog, build a life where the bottle has no place. The trick isn't in resisting what you fear, but in finding what matters and fixing your eyes on it like the last lit window on a dark street.

"Look where you want to go, not where you're afraid to go." This mantra is drilled into riders at the Motorcycle Safety Foundation and the California Superbike School, where target fixation can mean the difference between staying upright or leaving the track on a stretcher.

The Stoics thrived by living this truth. Marcus Aurelius didn't waste ink warning against weakness – he pointed unwaveringly toward strength. Epictetus didn't obsess over failure. He urged focus on duty – on doing what reason and character demand. They understood what every rider learns sooner or later: The body follows the eyes. The mind's no different.

So when the anxiety comes, don't whisper, "Don't panic." Say, "Breathe." When procrastination slithers in, don't groan, "Don't waste time." Open the file. Write the first sentence. Move.

When the old anger flares, don't feed it with *Don't lose your temper*. Pour it into the work, into the road, into the next right thing.

You'll drift. Of course you will. Christ knows I have – mid-chapter, mid-relationship, mid-Tuesday while the world tests my last nerve. Perfection isn't the goal. The return is. That quiet moment when you notice your gaze has slipped, and gently steer it back.

The road doesn't care about your intentions. The page is indifferent to your dreams. They respond only to where you point yourself, turn after stubborn turn. So point somewhere worth going. Then commit.

The rest? Just mechanics.

Riding teaches focus in its purest form – immediate and unforgiving. Fixate on the edge, and you'll drift toward it. Stare at the abyss, and you'll find yourself there. But anchor your vision on the vanishing point – where the road still curves ahead – and your body, your machine, your path will follow.

It's more than technique. It's rhythm. Tension and release. Seeing and responding. The tarmac teaches you to match your speed to what's visible, not what you hope lies beyond the bend. There are worse ways to live.

Your brain makes a terrible GPS. It doesn't do negatives, it clings to pictures. Tell it "Don't crash," and it hears and sees "CRASH HERE." Feed it fear, and it'll map routes through avoidance. Fuel it with resentment, and it'll loop you through the same dead ends. But set a clear destination – not with force, but clarity – and you begin navigating toward something true.

We spoke earlier about choosing your line. But selection means nothing if your eyes keep drifting to the ditch. So ask yourself: What commands your attention? What colour are your thoughts?

The road doesn't respond to your hopes. It follows your focus. So look where you want to go. And if you end up in the gravel? Brush yourself off, spit out the blood if you must, and fix your eyes more fiercely next time.

Chapter 8

No One Rides Alone

"We are waves of the same sea, leaves of the same tree, flowers of the same garden."
— Attributed to Seneca

YOU THINK YOU'RE DOING it alone.

Helmet on, ignition ticking, a single line carved into open road. And from the outside, it *does* look solitary – almost monastic. Just you, your thoughts, and the sound of your own engine. A clean break from conversation, obligation, complication. The whole world shrunk to mirrors, tarmac, and sky.

But it's a lie. Or at least, a half-truth – like most romantic ideas are.

That feeling of independence you love? It's held up by a hidden scaffolding. Your bike was designed by people you'll never meet. Your riding jacket stitched by someone whose name you'll never know. The fuel in your tank passed through refineries, ports, pumps, all managed by hands and minds far beyond your own. And the road – this strip of freedom you're gliding across – was surveyed, laid, and maintained by a civic ecosystem that probably couldn't care less about motorcycles, and yet here you are.

Even the very idea that you're a "lone rider" is, in truth, a shared fantasy. Because somewhere – out there or back home – someone taught you to ride. Someone once waited at the other end of the phone while you figured out how to change a tyre. And someone, possibly very recently, waved you off with a look that said, *Please don't die doing this.*

So no, you're not really doing it alone. You're just far enough ahead of the crowd to mistake the silence for solitude.

In Chapter 6, we discussed the Stoic understanding of *sympatheia* – the belief that everything is interconnected. Not in a vague, tree-hugging, everything-happens-for-a-reason sort of way. This is a grounded, practical philosophy: What benefits the whole, benefits the part. Or to borrow Marcus Aurelius's phrasing, "What is not good for the hive is not good for the bee."[69] We might like to think we're the bee. Independent, self-directed. But we're still flying with pollen from flowers we didn't plant.

This chapter is about the quiet ties that hold us up. The mentors who appear without ceremony. The strangers who step in, not because they owe us anything, but because someone once did the same for them. It's about what happens when we stop pretending strength means standing alone. We'll look at grease-stained acts of grace and at what it means to be human in a world that keeps trying to sell us the myth of the lone wolf. (Spoiler: Wolves hunt in packs.)

The Baton That Bound Us

You can do all the talking you like about rugged independence. About going it alone, about standing on your own two feet, about never needing anyone. But eventually, something happens to remind you you're not quite as self-contained as you thought.

Sometimes it's philosophical. Other times it's mechanical.

Like when your bike won't start outside a crumbling Italian petrol station at 7 a.m. You jiggle the key, you tap the dash, you pretend that frowning at it harder might change the outcome. It doesn't. You're staring down a 200-kilometre stretch of mountain pass with no mobile signal, no mechanic, and no clue – until someone in a battered Fiat pulls up, shrugs in Italian, and starts helping you bump-start it uphill. No questions asked. No invoice offered. Just grease and goodwill.

This is what the Stoics understood – the idea that we're part of a larger whole, that your pain is never yours alone, your triumphs not entirely self-made, and your freedom always subtly entangled with someone else's effort. To the modern ear, *sympatheia* might sound suspiciously like a team-building slogan or an ad for soy milk. But the ancient Stoics meant it seriously, and lived it rigorously. The point of life, said Zeno, the original Stoic, was not just to live in line with your own nature, but to live in line with *nature as a whole* – to be in harmony with the greater order.[70]

This wasn't sentimentality. It was structure. You were part of a city. A household. A species. You shared air, bread, law, and fate. Marcus Aurelius reminded himself daily that the good of the hive must outweigh the whims of the bee. It wasn't virtue unless it helped others. It wasn't strength unless it served the whole.

Fast forward a few thousand years and science has caught up. We're built to belong. When you're hugged, helped, or genuinely heard, your brain registers it as a reward. Social connection feels good because it's supposed to. Being excluded, on the other hand, triggers the same brain regions as physical pain.[71] That ache in your chest after a cold shoulder isn't imagined. It's neurological. You're wired for fellowship. Your survival depends on it. So does your happiness.

Of course, few things test this interdependence quite like an international motorbike relay.

It started with five words in a Facebook message: *Do you need any help?* I didn't know it then, but that one question would set a series of wheels in motion – real and metaphorical. Within four weeks, I was planning the Italian leg of the largest women's motorcycle relay the world had ever seen. I couldn't speak the language, wasn't even in the country, and yet I found myself mapping routes, rallying riders, and stepping into a role that would change the direction of my life.

The Women Riders World Relay (WRWR) was never just about riding. It was a call to connection – a way to show the world just how many women ride, and to give courage to the ones who didn't yet believe they could. In a culture where motorcycling is still seen as "a man's thing," WRWR handed the baton to women who might never have joined a group ride on their own. And the industry couldn't ignore it. Hundreds of women, country after country, handing a baton from one continent to the next. We weren't just riding. We were being seen.

I had joined the mission instinctively. Not because I needed attention from manufacturers or media, but because I remembered what it was like to hesitate. To wonder whether I'd be welcome. I'd been on testosterone-fuelled rides that made me question whether I belonged. But I'd also ridden with men and women whose generosity and patience lifted me. WRWR felt like a chance to offer that same lift to someone else.

Italy needed help. Their relay ambassador had stepped down. So I stepped in.

I had no contacts, but I had a will. Riders began to trickle in – some local, some from abroad. Then a breakthrough: Rosaria Fiorentino joined the team. A powerhouse of Italian motorcycling, she knew everyone. She opened doors, introduced us to sponsors, and before long we had a cross-country route, fourteen riders from four nations, and the start of something extraordinary.

To get there, though, I first had to survive the ride to Menton.

I'd set off solo from Troyes, determined to make it in time for the French handover. It was my longest day on a bike – over 900 km – and by nightfall I was crawling up the dark, twisting D2566 to the campsite above Sospel. Cold, knackered, and half-blind with fatigue, I'd turned off my audiobook to concentrate.

Unfortunately, it had other ideas. . . .

I'd been listening to *Jupiter's Travels*, Ted Simon's brilliant and often hilarious account of riding 126,000 km through 45 countries. Witty, insightful – and entirely inappropriate for the moment it sprang back to life without warning, somewhere near the summit.

And not gently. Suddenly I was treated to an enthusiastic retelling of Ted's, shall we say, intimate interlude – full of soft skin and milky breasts – just as I was white-knuckling through blind corners with headlights pressing behind me. I shouted, "Cancel! Close book!" at Siri, who, like all good assistants in moments of crisis, ignored me completely.

So I rode on, cheeks red, heart racing for all the wrong reasons, and burst out laughing at the absurdity of it all. Maybe a bit of tension relief wasn't the worst thing. To this day, a sharp bend in the road gives me a strangely warm glow.

We met in Menton for the baton handover from France, and rode east across Italy to Slovenia. Over two days, we covered nearly 1,000 km – coastal curves, high passes, lake roads, and city traffic – each mile stitched together with laughter, mechanical issues, late arrivals, and pastries. At every stop, we were met with cake, coffee, cameras, and kindness. Dealerships waved us in like queens. Mechanics checked our bikes, restaurateurs posed for photos, strangers clapped from the street.

It wasn't all smooth. I dropped my bike on a gravel monastery path – high on a steep hill with only a narrow, winding track to reach it. What we didn't realise was there was nowhere to park at the top. By the time I arrived, near the back of the pack, there was no space to stop and a brutal camber to manage. Apparently, I fell gracefully. I *do* fall well – an early skill from Judo at age six.

We got lost. We ran late. We were sweaty, sometimes overwhelmed. But no one got left behind. We helped each other up. We made decisions together. And when someone rode faster or further than they ever had before, we celebrated.

You can discipline your thinking all you want. You can meditate, self-improve, eat enough flaxseed to grow roots – but if you're doing it only for yourself, you've missed the point.

Connection isn't a detour from the path. It *is* the path.

The last night of the Italian leg, we reached the border with Slovenia well after dark. We were hours late. We were exhausted. We were slightly sunburnt in weird shapes. But the Slovenian riders were there waiting, lined up like sentries. When we handed them the baton, they clapped, hugged, wept. Not because we were important. But because *this* was.

That baton wasn't just a symbol. It was a carrier of stories. Of intentions. Of something ancient and tender that refuses to die – our need to be part of something larger than ourselves. The whole thing reminded me of an old Zen line: "The wave does not see itself as separate from the sea."

Marcus would have understood that.

We weren't messengers. We were the message.

WRWR wasn't just a relay. It was a reminder that sisterhood is alive and well. That courage is contagious. That leadership doesn't always look like someone at the front – it often looks like someone in the middle, quietly checking no one's dropped off the back.

I'll never forget those Italian women. Their joy, their spirit, their flair for the dramatic. Or the sound of our engines echoing through the Strada della Forra like Valkyries on a mission. We weren't riding for ego or glory. We were riding to say: We're here. And we ride too.

So if you've ever felt like you don't belong, if you've ever worried you're an outlier or impostor, take this with you: No one rides alone. Not really. The road is solitary, yes. But the journey never is.

Someone paved it before you. Someone will ride it after you. And if you're lucky, someone's riding it with you now.

The Stoics were right. You weren't made to go it alone. You were made to go together.

Even if it takes a Facebook message, a mountain pass, and a dented baton to realise it.

Cold Starts and Warm Welcomes

There's a kind of morning that quietly tells you: You're not ready for this. Cold air on bare neck, stiff hands on handlebars, the thrum of doubt just louder than the engine. That was me, easing onto the M20 with the grace of a wardrobe on wheels, heading toward the STOP 24 Services at Folkestone. It was early spring, still winter in spirit. The sun had barely broken the horizon. A bitter wind cut straight through my thin Eaglerider jacket – more suited to California highways than freezing British mornings. My first European guided trip from England to France with Magellan Motorcycle Tours, on a bright red Indian Scout, and I already felt like I'd made a mistake.

I'd taken the spot last-minute along with my mate Spider, a.k.a. Ray, who I'd met the previous year on a ride through Death Valley and Yosemite. His friend Mark was a motorcycle tour guide with Magellan and had tipped him off about a couple of discounted places that had opened up after someone dropped out. I said yes before fear had time to talk me out of it. That's usually how I get myself into these things.

I arrived late, despite planning not to. The frost had slowed me more than expected. Another lesson. As I pulled in, the group was already gathered – coffee in gloved hands, boots planted wide, voices rising and falling in easy rhythm. A row of GSs, Triumphs, and KTMs gleamed under grey skies. I scanned for another cruiser. Nothing. No other Scouts. No other outliers. Just me.

I parked beside one of the bikes, took off my helmet, and immediately regretted it. Helmet hair, stiff neck, and zero idea what to do next. Everyone else looked like they knew what they were doing. I stood there pretending to check something on my bike, willing myself to disappear.

Then Nene appeared.

Like an angel, this big, beautiful woman with a smile wider than the Grand Canyon and a vibe that said "I'm huggable" walked straight up to me and introduced herself. It changed everything.

Suddenly, I felt included. Seen. Welcomed.

Then came Paul. Then Spider appeared. Then Billy. Then Storm. One by one, each person chipped away at the edges of my doubt until the panic that had gripped my chest eased into something quieter. Safe. Seen. Belonging.

That moment crystallised something I've felt again and again since:

If you ride, you don't ride alone.

There's a community out there. A tribe. One that doesn't care what you ride – only that you showed up.

Now, I'm not going to get all sentimental and tell you that moment was magical. But, chemically? It might as well have been. Oxytocin, the so-called "bonding hormone," spikes during warm social connection. When someone sees you – really sees you – your nervous system clocks it before you do. Blood pressure drops. Breathing slows. You go from threat mode to trust mode. A single moment of welcome can undo hours of stress.[72] Better than vitamins. Possibly better than therapy. And certainly more immediate.

We're built to fit together, not to function alone.

But belonging, for the Stoics, was never about joining a club or matching the uniform. It wasn't about being liked. It was about alignment. Zeno, the founder of the school, described the goal of life as living *in agreement* – with nature, with reason, with the whole. That agreement includes others. We are fragments of a shared order. Our job is to find how we move in harmony with it.

The irony, of course, is that we tend to think strength is standing apart. That independence means freedom. Epictetus, the grumpiest of Stoics, would disagree. "No man is free who is not master of himself," he said, "but no man is whole who is not part of others."

Riding with others reminds you of that. There's a collective rhythm that kicks in. Helmets snap shut in sequence. Engines fire like a call-and-response. When you're riding in a group, you can feel it – that odd, sacred thrum Émile Durkheim once called *collective effervescence*. The feeling of being lifted into something larger than yourself, not by disappearing, but by being fully seen, and joined.[73]

We all crave tribe. Not in the corporate team-building sense. In the bone-deep, cave-painting, pass-the-firewood kind of way. We need to know we're part of something that would notice if we were gone. That someone, somewhere, would keep a seat for us.

That day, at the motorway services, I learned this: You don't need to belong on paper. You don't need the right bike or the right gear. You need one person – one Nene – to reach out and make space.

Invisible Hands

Just before the engine kicks in, everything stills. You're perched on the bike, helmet strapped, gloves snug, eyes locked on the road ahead. It's quiet, but not empty. Behind you – though you can't see them – are the invisible hands.

The ones who got you here. We all have them and I'm lucky enough to say I struck gold with mine. Ray – Spider – was the first to steady me. Ex-Navy bomb disposal diver, endlessly prepared, and with a bike so clean it practically sparkled. He always had the right tool, the right words, and a deadpan line that could disarm the tensest moment. While I was still wobbling through corners and second-guessing myself, he never made a fuss – just quietly passed on the kind of hard-won wisdom that sticks. Usually with a joke, sometimes with a look. Always spot-on.

Then there was Billy – fire in his belly, rain on his face – who trained me up as a tour guide and made damn sure I stopped tiptoeing through corners. Even in the freezing, sideways rain of Germany, he'd shout, "Lean in! Tilt your head! Trust it!" He pushed me past my hesitation, past the voice that always said *play it safe*.

And when it all went to shit at Bonneville – when the bike died and I stood there on the salt flats, almost in tears, thinking the whole thing was over – my phone rang. It was Billy. I didn't even get a word out before he snapped down the line in that thick Scottish growl, full of fire and gravel: "This is not how your story ends! You hear me? You don't quit here. You bloody rise."

He believed when I didn't. And that – *that* – kept me going.

And Mick and Becci Ellis – a formidable husband and wife team. Becci holds the current female world record for a standing mile on a conventional motorbike: 264.1mph, on a machine Mick designed and built. Their calm guidance and rock-solid hand of friendship gave me the courage to chase speed records – and the belief that I just might belong on the start line. I owe them so much.

Add to that the women who inspired me in so many ways – Claire Elsdon, Hayley Bell, Lois Pryce, Shonagh Ravensdale, Jacqui Furneaux. I could name more and still not scratch the surface. Trailblazers, each in their own way.

Then there are the people I've ridden with on tours – strangers at the start, friends by the end. Karen and Jim. Paul and Nene, Miles and Zoe. Heck, I even got a tattoo with Karen and two other riders I'd only met a few days earlier. We're dragon siblings now.

That's what sharing miles with people does to you. It leaves a mark – in more ways than one. Each of them gave me as much or more than I gave them.

And beyond them, the ones whose names I'll never know – women and men who carved their own paths long before the rest of us even realised we could. The ones who rode before the roads had names at all.

That's the invisible architecture of belonging. You don't always see it. But it holds you up all the same. "You find yourself only in the midst of others," as American educator and author Adam Robinson put it. He emphasises that life is a game, and within it, connection is essential for both success and personal fulfillment.

Robinson urges us to create joy for others in every interaction – not as a tactic, but as a way of being. Make things fun. Bring delight. Focus less on outcomes and more on connection.

So next time you feel like an outsider – and you will, because we all do – remember this: Your place isn't earned by credentials. It's revealed in connection.

And if you can be someone else's Nene – do. Not because it's heroic. But because it's human.

The Stoics would approve. They were quite clear on this point: We are not self-made. Marcus Aurelius wrote: "We are made for cooperation, like feet, like hands, like eyelids."[74] Interdependence wasn't weakness; it was design.

Zeno took it further. He said the aim of life is to live in harmony, not only with our own nature but with the nature of the whole. Which is quite a nice way of saying: Don't try to ride through life solo. You're part of something.

The thing is, we often forget. Especially when life – or riding – feels like a solo mission. But every time you've asked a question, every time someone's shown you the right tool, every time a stranger offered directions, advice, or encouragement – you've experienced what I call the Invisible Hands Effect. A quiet web of support, often unseen, but always present.

This support isn't abstract. It's deeply physiological. A warm welcome calms the nervous system. A single moment of inclusion – like Nene's hug at a freezing Folkestone petrol station – can trigger a ripple effect that lowers anxiety, restores confidence, and signals to your body that it's safe to relax. In other words, that hug may have done more than any vitamin ever could.

Sociologist Émile Durkheim called it collective effervescence – that electricity you feel when you're part of something bigger. That's what group rides offer. It's not just the thrum of engines or the geometry of machines moving in sync. It's the primal reassurance that you belong to something – something real, and human, and bigger than your self-doubt.

We often speak of freedom as independence. But real freedom – soul-deep freedom – arises not from being separate, but from being supported. Not from riding alone, but from riding together.

So how do we honour those invisible hands?

Start with the nod. Acknowledge every rider you pass. It's a small habit, but it builds the muscle for connection. One second of shared humanity on an open road. A reminder that you're part of something bigger.

Buy a coffee for the person behind you. No reason. Just because you can. If they ask why, say, "Because." If they try to thank you, ask them to pass it on.

I first did this in France, after hearing the idea from another legend, Sue Hollis. It was just after 9 a.m. I walked into a little café – still in full bike gear – and the place went quiet. Two blokes were already on wine, a few others sipping espresso.

I'd promised myself I'd go through with it. I looked around and spotted an older gent in the corner, reading *Le Monde* or something like it. His cup was empty. So, in my best (and truly terrible) French, I asked the café owner if I could buy him another. He shrugged. "*Oui*."

It caused a stir. The old guy looked from his cup to me, completely baffled. I said, "*Pour vous*." He frowned, then started speaking rapidly to a woman nearby. No one spoke much English, so I pulled out Google Translate. She read the message:

"Please accept this as a gift. If you'd like to thank me, please do the same for someone else someday."

She smiled. Then spoke. The room lit up – laughter, chatter, a ripple of something shared. The old man raised his cup and gave me a wink.

Worth it. Even if they all thought, *Ah, the English – completely mad.*

One thing I've learned: The person who gives always gets back more. It's the law of reciprocity – and it's a real thing. Another way to give back is by passing on a skill. Someone took the time to teach you – how to read a corner, adjust a chain, or pack a roll bag so it stays put at speed. Share that. It doesn't need to be formal. Maybe it's a quick tip at a petrol station or a reply in a group chat. What matters is keeping the thread going.

For non-riders, do a tribe audit. Think of three people who've helped you – mentors, supporters, the ones who showed up when you didn't know you needed it. Then thank one. Just one. A quick message is enough. You don't need a speech. Just let them know they mattered.

And offer micro-mentorship. Say yes to someone newer than you. Not with a script, just with attention. Share the answer to a question you once asked. Give fifteen minutes. Open a door you once found locked.

That's how we honour them. By not letting what they gave stop with us.

Now, you may have noticed I haven't said much about how I ended up with the Hayabusa, or the fate of the red LPG (propane) bike that didn't survive its first taste of salt at Bonneville. That part of the story is complicated. But this chapter isn't about that.

What matters more is how I got here at all. It was the friend who saved me from dehydration in Death Valley and told me I was good enough to ride again.

It was the WRWR relay that carried me across Italy – powered by Rosaria's relentless organisation and energy.

It was Talan, at The Bike Experience, who gave me the confidence – and the quiet wisdom – to take my first run on the sand at Pendine.

And the pub friends from Demon Designs – whose racing name sounded far scarier than they were – who taught me how not to crash immediately.

Yes, I took a leap. I said yes to jumping on a heavyweight bike and deciding to ride through Death Valley and the West Coast of America. That was mine to own. But everything that followed? That was other people.

Suzanne, Vito, Waldo, Larry, Dale – people who had no reason to help me when the engine on that red LPG superbike blew out on the salt flats. But they did. They gave their time, their tools, and their encouragement. No agenda. No applause.

I've never been more humbled in all my life.

It wasn't me – not really. It was all of them.

And that's the thing. Every mile I've ridden since, I've carried them all with me. Not in a sentimental way. Not in a grand, cinematic montage. Just . . . quietly. In my posture. In the way I help someone load a pannier. In the way I nod at another rider. In the way I pause before starting the engine and feel them all there – behind me, beside me, ahead of me.

The ones who smiled.

The ones who nodded.

The ones who reached out their gloved hand and welcomed me into something ancient and unspoken.

I may look alone on the road.

But I never am.

And neither are you.

Chapter 9

Ride With Virtue

"Heroes and cowards feel the same fear. They just respond differently."
— Cus D'Amato

T.E. LAWRENCE RODE ALONE most mornings. Long before most of Britain stirred their tea, he was out on the winding Dorset lanes, wind slicing across his face, throttle low, gears deliberate. He wasn't riding for show. There was no camera crew, no curated content, no hashtags. Just a man and his Brough Superior – a machine he once called "the Rolls-Royce of motorcycles" – cutting through the morning mist like it might teach him something if he went far enough, fast enough, deep enough into his own silence.

And it did.

In his book *The Mint*, Lawrence reflected the sensation of riding not as conquest, but as a form of release – into solitude, simplicity, and something larger than himself.[75] The world could be loud, political, absurd. But on the bike, things simplified. Right hand, left clutch, eyes up, breath steady. He found discipline there. Not the parade-ground kind. The internal sort. Self-rule.

It's this kind of quiet, unphotogenic virtue that Stoicism celebrates. Not the polished stuff of speeches, but the smaller, unseen acts: helping a stranger fix a flat, slowing down so the new rider doesn't get left behind, resisting the urge to explain how brilliant you are at U-turns. Integrity, said the Stoics, is not for display. It's for use. As Epictetus reminds us – philosophy isn't to be spoken. It's to be lived.

Which brings us, gently, to you.

You've likely admired virtue more than once: the medic who goes back into the chaos when they could leave, the friend who owns their mistake without deflection, the stranger who steps in, quietly, when someone needs help. We look at those people and feel something ancient stir in us – that's what I should do. That's who I want to be. And yet, when the moment comes, we hesitate. We explain. We overthink. We keep scrolling.

Why?

Because virtue demands effort, not applause. It's inconvenient. It costs energy, time, pride. Sometimes you'll be late. Sometimes you'll look odd. Occasionally you'll help someone who won't thank you. Stoicism doesn't mind. In fact, it expects that. Marcus Aurelius, while running an empire, reminded himself daily that people would be rude, selfish, ungrateful – and that his task was to help them anyway.[76] Not because they deserved it, but because *he* wanted to remain himself.

In this chapter, we'll ride with the four Stoic virtues:

Courage – the strength to face your fear and still throw a leg over the bike.

Wisdom – knowing when to ease off the throttle, or to say, "I don't know."

Justice – the choice to help when no one's watching.

Temperance – the restraint to stop before ego becomes a liability.

These aren't grand philosophical ideals. They're survival skills. They keep you upright – literally, on the road, and figuratively, when life kicks out your stand and the tarmac looks far too close.

We'll meet modern riders too. One who delivers blood samples at midnight without fanfare. Another who mentors disabled riders to reclaim agency after accidents. And you'll meet yourself – or at least a version of you that might begin to ask, not "What do I believe?" but "What do I do when no one's looking?"

Lawrence wasn't trying to be a Stoic. But he rode like one. And perhaps you already do too — in those small moments of restraint, resolve, and kindness. This chapter is simply a reminder: You don't need to quote Epictetus to live like him. You just need to show up — calmly, consistently, and consciously.

Helmet on. Mirrors checked. Let's begin.

The Four Virtues: Riding When No One's Watching

The Stoics didn't believe in style over substance. In fact, they didn't care much for style at all. They didn't stand on podiums. They walked in markets. They stitched their philosophy not into speeches, but into the hems of daily life. They rode, so to speak, with their boots dusty and their engines warm.

Virtue, for them, wasn't grand or rare. It was what kept you steady when everything around you started to wobble. Like suspension on a long ride, it absorbs the jolt and steadies the frame — not because anyone's clapping, but because it's the only way to keep going without losing the plot.

Take *courage*, the first and perhaps least glamourised of virtues once you remove the Hollywood gloss. Courage, in Stoic thought, doesn't always look like charging in. More often, it looks like getting back on the bike after an accident – slowly, awkwardly, palms sweating inside the gloves. It's not confidence. It's conviction. I remember a woman I met through The Bike Experience – she was paralysed from the waist down after a crash. And yet, there she was, learning to ride again, modified controls and all, asking simply, *What else can I do that I was told I could never do again?* Not fearless. But forward.

Wisdom is less thrilling to market. There's no merchandise for knowing when to throttle back. But survival – on the road and off – depends on it. A novice rider learns this fast. Corners don't care about your ego. And neither does a wet descent on loose gravel. Wisdom is what kicks in when instinct says go faster and experience says, *You'll regret it.* It's the quiet voice that says, "Not today," when everyone else is saying, "Go on, just once." The Stoics would nod. Wisdom isn't knowing everything – it's knowing yourself.

Justice isn't always easy to define, especially outside courtrooms. But you've seen it. It's the Blood Biker who rides across town in the early hours with a transplant sample – unpaid, unseen, and completely necessary. Or the quiet determination of those in the Women Riders World Relay, handing the baton from one continent to the next, just to prove women belong on bikes. No one's getting rich. No one's looking for glory. They're just doing the next right thing. For the Stoics, justice meant contribution. A life larger than the self.

And then, *temperance*. The most overlooked virtue of the four, possibly because it's the least Instagrammable. No one gets likes for restraint. But it might just be the one that saves your life. Not overtaking when it's not quite clear. Not maxing out your speed because someone behind is too close. Temperance is what keeps your ego from oversteering the moment. It's the virtue that knows the difference between thrill and risk and chooses not to gamble with either.

These virtues aren't aspirational slogans. They're *practical tools*. The Stoics weren't preaching sainthood. They were suggesting a way to stay intact. Think of them not as medals, but maintenance. No one praises a well-tuned carburettor. But you notice when it goes wrong.

Mark Manson puts it more bluntly: "Action isn't the effect of motivation; it's the cause."[77] You don't feel brave, and then ride. You ride, and discover you were braver than you thought. Virtue doesn't need to be felt before it's acted. In fact, waiting for the feeling often guarantees it never comes.

The Stoics saw this. They didn't wait for inspiration. They acted rightly *because* it was right. George Washington embodied this spirit, valuing duty over recognition and striving to serve the greater good without seeking personal praise. In his 1796 *Farewell Address* – his final public speech as president – he emphasised putting the nation's interests above all else, showing a quiet discipline and commitment to principle. That's the idea.

So if you've been waiting to feel ready, or brave, or kind, stop. Do the thing. The feeling may follow. Or it may not. But either way, you've kept the bike upright when the road got rough. And that, quietly, is everything.

You're not here to be perfect. Just present. Engaged. Upright. One mile, one choice, one pause-for-breath at a time.

Virtue isn't a show. It's a direction. Keep riding in it.

Virtue in Motion

It started simply enough. I'd retired, had a bit more time on my hands, and didn't want to waste it. I'd recently fallen back in love with motorcycling and began to wonder: Could this thing I loved also be put to use? Could I ride with purpose, not just pleasure?

One evening, down the pub with my neighbour Val, I spotted a bright red motorbike in the car park, covered in the word *BLOOD*. It looked like it had taken a wrong turn out of a Bond film. I assumed someone had crashed and labelled the evidence. But Val leaned over and said, "That's a Blood Bike." As though this explained everything.

It didn't, of course. But curiosity did what curiosity does. A few questions later and I'd uncovered a quiet nationwide operation: volunteers on motorcycles, riding day and night to deliver urgent medical supplies – blood, plasma, baby milk, even surgical tools – to NHS hospitals across the UK. No sirens. No salaries. Just a commitment to help.

That was me hooked. I signed up to SERV (Service by Emergency Volunteers) Surrey and London branch after passing my IAM (Institute of Advanced Motorists) qualification. There was no epiphany, no heavenly choir. Just a small, deliberate decision to say yes. And like most good decisions, I only understood its impact in hindsight.

From there, the road took unexpected turns. Someone mentioned *The Bike Experience* – a track-day programme that helps disabled riders get back on two wheels, often after life-changing injuries. I went to one event out of curiosity and left changed. There, I watched a man with one arm and no legs suit up, swing onto a modified bike, and ride a lap with such joy it made you forget everything you thought you knew about limits. At the end, he asked the instructor: "What else have I been told I can't do?"

There it was: courage, justice, wisdom, and temperance. The four Stoic virtues, embodied in one quiet question.

The Stoics never said virtue was about spectacle. It's not about the big moment. It's about the small, deliberate acts that shape character over time. The Bike

Experience doesn't run on pity – it runs on belief. In agency. In dignity. In the idea that everyone, no matter their starting point, deserves the chance to act freely and fully. That's justice. Not an abstract concept, but a lived, practical ethic. It's not about rescuing someone. It's about making sure they don't have to be rescued again.

Another yes, another door. I found myself working with The Soroptimists, a network of women committed to empowering girls globally. Then came a trip to Tanzania to help a friend, Claire, with a women-led motorcycle repair school. Then WRWR – the Women Riders World Relay – and somehow, almost accidentally, an invitation to Bonneville Salt Flats.

The bike didn't make it past one run, of course. You might know that part. But the more interesting part was what happened next.

We were sitting in the car park of the Nugget motel in Wendover – beer in hand, dust on our boots, a barbecue crackling away on a battered grill. It wasn't glamorous. The Nugget is a budget casino hotel that straddles the Utah–Nevada border, built over one of the oldest gaming licences in America. Wendover Will – the world's largest mechanical cowboy – stands just down the road, grinning into the desert sky. But that night, under the neon hum and starlight, it felt like the centre of the world.

A group of Americans I'd met barely twenty-four hours earlier were already calling it a "consolation party". Somewhere between the beers and the burgers, I told them what had brought me to Bonneville. That for me, this wasn't just about speed – it was about story. I'd come to write about what's possible at any age, if you're just willing to say yes. That was what hit me hardest – not losing the run, but losing the reason.

Then something shifted. One of them said, "So get another bike."

Another pulled out a phone and started scrolling through eBay listings.

It felt like wishful thinking. Most of the bikes they found were hundreds of miles away, and Bonneville isn't exactly down the road from anywhere. It's hot, hostile, and mostly empty. The mood hovered somewhere between hopeful and ridiculous.

Then – a flash of white on a screen.

"Stop scrolling," I said. Then again, firmer: "That's the one."

I don't know where it came from – I just knew. Something in the shape of the bike, the line of the tank. I had the strange sense that I was seeing the future.

It was in Salt Lake City. A hundred miles away. The only bike even remotely close enough to make this dream possible. A Hyabusa Gen II. And from that moment on, a chain reaction began.

These once-strangers from the Nugget car park carried me like a crowd carries a singer from the back of the stadium to the stage.

Suzanne and Vito immediately took charge of the practicalities – arranging to view the bike the next day, hiring a trailer to get it from Salt Lake City to Wendover. I, of course, had no address to register it to, no clue how to buy a bike in the States, let alone how to insure one. But they just got to work.

Getting a bike to the flats was one thing. Getting it race-legal was another. There was a rule book as thick as your arm – pages of dos and don'ts. Mirrors had to be removed. The battery needed bolting down. A kill switch had to be fitted. Red tape applied to white panels, in case the bike ended up sideways on the salt. Easier to spot the bits when the marshals came looking.

On and on it went. But the BBQ heroes? They stepped up to the plate.

Those guys gave up their entire evening – which was probably meant for more beer drinking – to rebuild a machine they'd never seen before, for a rider they barely knew, with no promise of reward. Waldo, Larry, Dale – names you won't know, but I carry them with me.

They taught me that virtue isn't an individual act. It multiplies. It passes from hand to hand like a torch.

I'll never forget what they did.

Virtue begets virtue.

The Stoics were clear about this. Character isn't proven when it's convenient. It's revealed when the stakes are high and the outcome uncertain. That's when justice is justice, not PR. That's when courage is courage, not bravado. When you show up for someone, not because it benefits you, but because it's the kind of person you want to be.

There's no applause at 3 a.m. when you're delivering plasma on a rain-slick A-road. No Instagram story. Just the hum of the engine and the knowledge that someone, somewhere, will wake up tomorrow because of a journey you made.

The Stoics wouldn't have asked for more. They believed that virtue was its own reward. That a good life wasn't measured by what you got, but by how often you chose the right thing when it would've been easier not to. As Epictetus put it, "Don't explain your philosophy. Embody it."

So that's what I try to do. Not always perfectly, not without the occasional grumble. But by saying yes. By asking, again and again, "Where can I help?"

And if you're reading this, maybe you've asked that question too. Maybe the answer's already waiting. Maybe you've just yet to say yes.

Science of Character

Most mornings, the alarm blares, and we grope for the snooze button like a hungover monk praying for mercy. Philosophy probably isn't the first thing on your mind. But it's there – quietly – beneath the coffee, the newsfeed, the commute. Because every day, you're making a choice: *What kind of person will I become?*

The Stoics knew the truth: Character isn't built in grand gestures, but in the moments no one sees. Now, this isn't the sort of virtue that wins awards. No one's going to pin a medal on you for not shouting at a slow driver. There's no knighthood for resisting the urge to post a witty but undermining comment online. But these are the battles that matter. The rest is just noise.

The ancient Stoics didn't view virtue as a grand ideal. They saw it as a daily discipline. Courage, temperance, wisdom, justice – these weren't abstract nouns. They were habits. Muscles you strengthen through repeated use. You act with integrity not for applause, but because you're training yourself to be the sort of person who does.

Modern science is catching up to what the Stoics already knew: that living with virtue isn't just good – it's good *for you*. People who volunteer regularly or consistently practice kindness tend to experience greater contentment and even live longer. Research links acts of altruism to lower inflammation, improved heart health, and a reduced risk of chronic illness.[78]

Take volunteering, for example. One study found that older adults who volunteered had a 24% lower risk of dying during the study period, even after accounting for differences in health and lifestyle.[79] In fact, volunteering is as powerful as quitting smoking or exercising regularly. The heart truly listens when you act from the heart.

And the evidence doesn't stop there. The Harvard Study of Adult Development – the longest-running study of its kind – discovered that the happiest lives aren't the most successful or exciting, but the ones that are most contributive.[80] It's as if we're wired for virtue.

Something lasting begins to take root when we practice virtue consistently. Let's call it the Virtue Loop: You act with integrity, which builds self-trust, and that self-trust strengthens your resolve for the next moment of choice. Repeat.

Virtue begets virtue – not through mysticism, but through biology, neurology, and behaviour. It's a feedback system. Each courageous choice, no matter how small, makes the next one easier. Choosing patience over impulse carves new grooves in your neural pathways. You begin to trust yourself, and when you do, you no longer need the world's applause to feel grounded.

That's the science. But let's not get too clinical. Philosophy lives in the practical. So let's talk about how to ride with virtue – on the bike or off.

Virtue as Daily Maintenance

If you ride, try the "10% rule". Dedicate 10% of your ride time to someone else. Mentor a new rider. Volunteer as a marshal. Escort someone on their first long ride. You don't need a cape – just a willingness to share the road with kindness. Then do a "mirror check": After each ride, ask: *Where did I choose courage over comfort today?* Was it overtaking more patiently than usual? Admitting a mistake on the group chat? Let that moment be your lodestar for tomorrow.

If you're not riding – or grounded for now – practice "micro-justice". Do one quiet act of kindness that goes unnoticed. Cover for a colleague without credit. Correct gently instead of shaming. Let someone off the hook even when you could press your advantage. These are the tiny stitches that hold society together. Or take on a "temperance trial": Pick one indulgence to forgo today – not as punishment, but as practice. No snacks between meals. No checking your phone after 9 p.m. No gossip. These trials teach you that freedom isn't the absence of limits – it's mastery over them. And finally, I call these "courage reps". Do one thing that makes you slightly uncomfortable – but aligns with your values. Speak up. Apologise first. Ask for help. It's how we stretch character without snapping it. Small lifts. Not dramatic, just necessary. It's how character grows: under slight tension, every day.

The Stoics never waited to feel virtuous. They acted, and let the virtue follow.

As W.H. Murray, a Scottish mountaineer and author known for his pioneering Himalayan expeditions, wrote in *The Scottish Himalayan Expedition*, "Until one is committed, there is hesitancy, the chance to draw back, always ineffectiveness . . . the moment one definitely commits oneself, then Providence moves too."[81]

Think about that: If you wait to feel ready, you may never begin. But the instant you take the leap – even a small one – you set off a chain reaction. Motivation, clarity, courage – they follow the action.

The Stoics understood this long before neuroscience confirmed it: Action precedes emotion. Seneca, especially, knew the mind could be fickle – sluggish in the morning, overconfident by night, and full of justifications in between. So he didn't wait for the right mindset. He made virtue a verb.

Want to be more courageous? Do the brave thing. Want to feel more generous? Give before you feel like it. Want to feel strong? Say no to something easy. The feeling trails the action, not the other way around.

You don't become virtuous by thinking about it. You become virtuous by riding it. One choice at a time. One micro-decision at a time. Over and over. Until one day, you realise you trust yourself. And that's a kind of freedom few people ever find.

The Road to Ourselves

No one tells you this when you buy your first bike, but you're not just signing up for two wheels and a few Sunday rides. You're joining a rolling meditation on who you are and how you live. Helmets conceal the faces, leathers hide the figures, but the road has a way of peeling back the layers. Eventually, every ride becomes a mirror.

The Stoics understood this long before motorcycles existed. To them, life was the journey *towards* the self, not *away* from it. The aim wasn't sainthood or serenity – it was integrity. Not the polished version of you that makes speeches or posts selfies, but the person who still does the right thing when no one's there to clap. Especially then.

That's what Marcus Aurelius meant when he wrote, "Waste no more time arguing about what a good person should be. Be one."[82] A philosopher-emperor, leading legions by day, journaling by candlelight at night. You might not run an empire, but you *do* run your own life. And you know, just as he did, that virtue isn't theory. It's practice.

You probably won't feel heroic when you adjust a new rider's mirrors without being asked. Or when you wait at a junction for the one falling behind. Or when you pick up someone else's litter in the car park because it was the right thing to do. But those are the moments that shape you. Small, silent, and utterly transformative.

Virtue isn't sainthood – it's showing up as your best rider, your best human, one mile at a time.

And no, you won't get it right every time. Neither did Seneca. He admitted as much. The Stoics never claimed perfection; they aimed for progress. They understood that the road was long, the weather unpredictable, and the engine sometimes temperamental. But they rode on anyway.

You might be asking, what's the point? Why bother when no one's looking, when recognition is rare and payoffs uncertain?

Because the payoff is *you*.

Act with integrity, and you start trusting yourself. Be just, and the world starts to feel more just. Say no when it's hard, and you build self-respect. Virtue doesn't guarantee outcomes, but it does guarantee self-possession. As Epictetus taught, true freedom comes from mastering yourself, not controlling the world around you: "No man is free who is not master of himself."[83]

It doesn't take much to start. Next time you gear up, ask yourself: *How can this ride serve more than just me?* Maybe you invite a newcomer. Maybe you ride a little slower so someone else doesn't feel left behind. Maybe you stop to offer directions when you're in a rush.

You'd be surprised how often those tiny acts ripple out. I've seen it in the way a gloved hand quietly adjusts a novice's helmet strap – firm, gentle, unquestioned. No fuss, no performance. Just care. That's virtue. And it spreads.

It reminds me of something the Roman philosopher Cato the Younger was known for. He wore the same cloak in public no matter the season, walked barefoot through Rome, and refused bribes with a shrug. People mocked him. But when the republic fell and chaos loomed, they remembered him. Because he'd stood steady when others wavered. He didn't become a hero by accident. He'd been rehearsing it in plain sight for years.[84]

Virtue isn't the loudest rider in the group. It's the one who notices who's struggling. The one who loops back without being asked. The one who checks your fuel tank when you forget. The one who shows up, again and again, even when no one's keeping score.

That sounds like who I want to be.

And if you're still reading this, it probably sounds like you, too.

PART FOUR

EXPANSION

The ride reveals you. Bit by bit. A straighter spine. More conviction in your voice. You shed what no longer fits, quietly and without regret.

Growth comes when you recognise where you've been and lean into what's becoming clearer. These chapters hold that stretch — the shift, the recalibration, the sense of alignment. It's not about chasing more. It's about meeting more of yourself and making space for what's already unfolding.

Chapter 10

Check Your Mirrors

"Men are like steel. When they lose their temper, they lose their worth."
— Chuck Norris

I WAS WHITE-KNUCKLED ON A blind bend in Wales, chasing someone else's definition of good riding. Out of my depth. Out of my line. Barely in control. Not because the road was too much, or the bike too powerful, but because I was trying to keep up with a story that didn't belong to me.

It wasn't the road I was riding. It was someone else's expectations. I wasn't listening to my instincts. I was listening to ego.

We don't like to admit it, but sometimes the most dangerous rider on the road isn't the one in front of you – it's the one inside your own helmet. That quiet voice that says, "Go on, show them." That whisper doesn't come from confidence. It comes from the need to be seen. To be approved of. To not fall behind.

Ego doesn't shout. It nudges. It's the one that says, *You're slowing the group down. . . . They'll think you're rubbish. . . . Better speed up, mate – prove them wrong.* It dresses itself as drive, ambition, pride. But what it really does is cloud your judgment.

When I came back to riding after twenty-four years off the bike, I thought it would feel like slipping into an old book. Pick up where I left off. A few pages in and I'd be right back in the groove, knees out, apex in sight, no drama.

It wasn't like that.

I was shaky. I'd passed my test back in 1990, back when you could legally ride a missile after weaving between cones in a parking lot. But I'd never really ridden. Not in any serious way. Not with purpose. Not with skill.

It wasn't until years later – under that wide Nevada sky on an Indian Scout – that something real clicked. Something deeper than nostalgia. Something that said, *This is who you are when no one's watching.* That cross-country ride across the States was a gift. Formation riding hides a lot. You just follow. Stay in the groove. You don't need to lead. You barely even need to think. As long as you keep formation, no one sees your limits.

But back in the UK, there was nowhere to hide.

My lines were sloppy. I looked down instead of ahead. Wobbled through corners. I made awkward, mumbled excuses at café stops. I was always the last to arrive, always slower than the pack. And I hated that.

So I started learning. Properly. I read books, made notes, drew diagrams. I pulled out flipcharts and sketched teapot-shaped motorcycles while trying to decode *Motorcycle Roadcraft*. I rewrote sections of *How to Be a Better Rider* as if I were studying for an exam. But more than anything, I kept riding. Every weekend. Through Surrey, Sussex, Kent. Always with riders who were better than I was.

After a few months, I started to feel solid. Confident. I thought I'd made real progress. So I joined a club ride to Snowdonia – twenty-five of us meeting just outside London, using the old drop-off system to stick together.

At first, it felt great. The bike was working with me. I was holding pace. But it didn't last long. Cracks started to show. My skill didn't match the confidence I'd been riding on. I got tense. Lost rhythm. One corner behind, one mistake away from going wide.

I clung to the back marker and tried to pretend I was fine. And then, like a lot of people with something to prove, I made the classic mistake: I sped up.

It just made things worse. I started blowing corners, braking late, pushing in the wrong places. I tried to make up time where it didn't matter and almost rode into someone at a petrol station. I can still see their brake light coming up too fast. Still feel my stomach drop. It's painful to remember.

But I didn't quit. I got honest. I wrote notes after every ride. Asked questions. Took things apart. I rode with people who made it look easy – and never made a show of it. I stopped caring what they rode. What mattered was *how* they rode.

My best riding mates now? They're brilliant. Quietly so. No bravado. No competition. Just people who help when you stall on a hill or drop your bike in a river – both of which I've done. That's where the real learning happens. That's how you grow.

Ask. Watch. Try. Repeat. Not to impress. To improve.

I don't fake it anymore. I don't bluff skill I haven't earned.

Marcus Aurelius nailed it when he wrote, "It never ceases to amaze me: we all love ourselves more than other people, but care more about their opinion than our own." That's ego in a single sentence.

So now – before every ride – I check my mirrors. Not just for traffic. I'm looking for the passenger I never invited. If I catch a glimpse – ego, sitting there, grinning like it knows better – I let it ride. But it stays in the back seat. It doesn't get to steer.

The Two Faces of Ego

Ask yourself a small question: Would you rather *be* a good rider – or be *seen* as one?

It sounds innocuous. Almost rhetorical. But it cuts deeper than it first appears. One answer is about craft. The other is about audience.

And ego? Ego always chooses audience.

The thing is, Ego doesn't just ride bikes. It shows up at work, at home, online. It's the voice in your helmet – or your head – that you'd do well to ignore. It doesn't shout. It whispers. Low and steady, with a tone that sounds like confidence but isn't. It flatters. Tells you you're sharper than instinct, quicker than your own reactions, smarter than gravity. And because it uses your voice, you believe it.

That's the trick. Ego never looks like the villain. It sounds like you. One minute it tells you, *You've been riding for thirty years – you've got this.* The next, it hisses, *You're falling behind. Don't let them see it.* First it pushes you to lean harder, ride faster, prove something. Then it wraps your pride in fear, convincing you that being slow is worse than being wrong.

Same voice. Same lie. Always performing. Always pressing.

That's ego. And it's one of the most dangerous things you can bring on a ride. More dangerous than wet roads, high crosswinds, blind corners. Because ego doesn't just ride with you – it wants the throttle. It wants control. It wants to decide what kind of rider you are, regardless of the truth.

The worst part? You hear it so often, you stop noticing. But once you do – once you really see it – you start riding differently. Not slower, but smarter. Not to prove anything, but to enjoy everything. You listen to the road instead of the noise in your head. You leave space. Between you and the next rider. Between fear and response. Between who you think you should be and who you actually are.

And the ride improves. It might be slower. But it's better.

Seneca wrote, "The greatest obstacle to living is expectancy, which depends upon the morrow and wastes today." Ego thrives on that future orientation – how you'll look, how you'll perform, how others will remember you. But riding, like living, happens now. And the road doesn't care how many miles you've logged.

Take something more literal. In the 1970s, a Triumph Bonneville T120 made 46 horsepower. A Honda CB750 put out 67. Both were considered serious bikes. Today, a modest commuter like the Kawasaki Ninja 650 makes the same. A Yamaha MT-09 hits 117. A Kawasaki Ninja H2 – if you've taken leave of your senses – delivers over 200, straight from the showroom.

You'd think numbers like that would give a rider pause.

And yet, the script at group rides rarely changes.

"I don't need advice from a twenty-something instructor."

"I've been riding since the '80s."

"Not wearing one of those bright vests – looks daft."

Then there's the one I used to believe: *"I'll show them I can keep up."*

Experience isn't the same as expertise. Socrates said it best: "The beginning of wisdom is admitting what you don't know." Motorcycling has a ruthless way of exposing exactly that – especially if you confuse time in the saddle with actual ability.

Maybe you passed your test back when it meant weaving through cones in a parking lot, a loop in second gear, and someone with a clipboard behind you. That doesn't mean you're ready for a 1000cc machine with electronics tuned for riders who know how to use them.

Statistically, returning riders are overrepresented in serious crashes. A 2008 Transport Research Laboratory report flagged overconfidence, poor hazard perception, and outdated technique. In 2023, the UK's Department for Transport confirmed that men aged thirty to fifty-nine – especially those returning after long breaks – are disproportionately involved in single-vehicle accidents, particularly in corners.

The machines have changed. Physics hasn't.

But this isn't a sermon. Just a nudge. One rider to another.

Check your mirrors – not just for traffic, but for that voice saying you've nothing left to learn. That voice wants the bars. Let it talk, but don't hand it the controls.

When I came back to riding after twenty-four years, I told myself I could still hack it. I joined that club ride to Snowdonia full of confidence and very little substance. I spent most of the day chasing people who weren't racing, cornering on nerves, and lying to myself about how badly I wanted to stop.

Then came the wake-up: One of the riders overtook me on a blind left-hander. Inches from my bar. I hadn't checked my mirror in all of five seconds. He must've closed the gap like a missile.

I steadied the bike. Took a breath. And asked: *What are we doing here?*

Why was he risking his one life just to get ahead of someone slower?

Why was I so desperate not to be the one holding people up?

That's when I slowed down. The chasing stopped. I told ego to sit in the back. I finished the ride at my own pace. When we reached our stop, I peeled off and headed home solo. Just me and the bike, laughing, singing, learning as I went.

That, I think, is what the Stoics meant by *amor fati* – the love of fate. Not just accepting your lane, but embracing it. Owning your pace. Riding your ride. Letting others pass, and still arriving whole.

Humility isn't about putting yourself down. It's about seeing yourself clearly. Not thinking less of yourself – just thinking about yourself less. That applies just as much off the bike.

So ask yourself:

What's ego whispering in your helmet today?

And what might change if you stopped listening?

The Difference Between Excellence and Validation

The Stoics inherited a powerful metaphor from the Cynics: *tuphos* – "mist" or "smoke" – a kind of mental fog. Not the good kind that rises off a Scottish loch at dawn, but the self-induced type that clouds judgment and breeds vanity. Zeno warned against this fog explicitly. Conceit, he argued, was the enemy of growth. If you think you've arrived, you stop walking. If you believe you've mastered the road, you forget to check the corners[85].

Socrates offered the antidote: keep asking questions. Especially the ones aimed at yourself. Especially when you're sure you already know the answer.

There's a certain kind of rider – and you've seen them – who buys the fastest bike they can afford, fits a tail tidy, deletes the baffles, and makes sure to blip the throttle extra loud when passing a group outside a pub. It's loud. It's flashy. And yes, you might admire the bike – the engineering, the paintwork, the sheer audacity of it. You might even flinch at the volume.

But let's not confuse spectacle with skill.

True excellence doesn't need to announce itself. It shows up in the rider who moves smoothly through a curve, who knows when to throttle on and when to hold back. It's quiet confidence, not noise. Precision over posturing. Mastery, not performance for the crowd.

Ego wants the loudest exhaust.

Excellence wants the cleanest line.

That's the difference between validation and mastery. One thrives on attention. The other doesn't need an audience.

In *Ego is the Enemy*, Ryan Holiday calls this the "student mindset."[86] It's the opposite of arrival. It's turning up to every ride with something to learn – especially when you think there isn't. It's asking someone younger how they take a hairpin. It's not flinching when they point out your weak right-handers. It's recognising that limits aren't flaws – they're entry points.

We forget that. Especially in a group.

There's something tribal about the café line-up. Bikes parked like cavalry. Helmets placed with precision. Conversation turns to coded status updates. "I came through the A272 this morning." "Took it at pace." "Scraped the pegs." No one says, "I was wobbly through the roundabouts and nearly stalled at the lights," even if that's exactly what happened. Because showing your work feels like showing weakness.

And ego hates that.

But here's the quiet truth: Restraint stands out more than performance ever will. Smooth riders catch your eye without trying. The ones who brake early. Roll on with patience. Never flinch. Never rush. There's a kind of grace in it. And it's usually earned the long way – through mistakes, recovered slowly and honestly.

Philosophy has a word for this: *sōphrosynē*. A kind of temperance. Emotional discipline. The ability to hold back even when you could push forward. Not from fear. But because you don't need to prove anything.

That's what wisdom looks like: knowing how to go unnoticed when part of you wants to be seen.

So ask yourself:

When you ride, who are you riding for?

Who's watching – and why does it matter?

If the answer is anyone other than you and the road ahead, it's time to recalibrate.

Good riders don't announce themselves. You notice them in the way they move. The way they corner. Calm. Quiet. Controlled. You see it in how they sit at a junction. You feel it in how they carry themselves. It's not loud. It's not dramatic. It's just good. And they rarely talk about it.

Maybe, like Socrates, they're more interested in your answer than their own.

When Ego Won't Yield

The thing about ego is that it doesn't often arrive with trumpets. It sidles in quietly, pretending to be confidence, grit, ambition, or even self-respect. You're in the middle of something – a meeting, a creative project, a ride – and then it whispers, "You should take the lead." "Don't let them outshine you." "Make sure they know what you're capable of." And before you realise it, you're not doing the thing for the sake of the thing anymore. You're performing.

The Stoics didn't talk about ego in modern terms, but they knew the voice. Seneca often wrote about it – that need to prove, to show, to grasp at validation. That urge to impress others? It's just ego delaying your peace. Zeno saw conceit as the enemy of wisdom. You can't learn if you're too busy pretending you already know. Socrates, of course, took this further than anyone. He built an entire method around the quiet power of asking questions instead of making declarations. He wasn't interested in seeming wise. He just wanted to find the truth. His genius wasn't in knowing the answers. It was in being unafraid to admit when he didn't.

This is the work of self-awareness: to notice the moment ego steps in and gently name it. "Ah," you say, "there's that voice again, wanting to be seen." You don't need to fight it. Just spot it. That's usually enough.

You'll meet this voice in many forms. It shows up when someone offers feedback you didn't ask for. It shows up when a colleague gets the credit. It shows up when you're tempted to share something – not because it's meaningful, but because you want the applause. You don't have to shut the voice down. Just don't let it steer. Take the wheel back.

The Stoics taught a second tool too: detachment. This isn't about cold indifference. It's about refusing to let praise or criticism determine your worth. You'll get advice in life, whether you want it or not – from bosses, friends, strangers on the internet. Some of it will contradict itself beautifully. You might hear one thing from someone who seems terribly wise, and the opposite from someone equally persuasive. Listen with patience. Let it all wash through. Something will stick eventually.

And yes, occasionally, you'll see that the advice-giver is speaking more for themselves than for you. Their ego might be driving the conversation. That's alright. You can see it, name it, and smile. Just try not to be too pleased with yourself for noticing – that's your ego slipping in the side door.

It's not just people that draw ego out. It's platforms, too. Social media rewards the loud. We've created a world where people live to be witnessed. There are those who post every moment of progress, every win, every act of kindness, not because they want to share the experience, but because they want recognition. There's nothing inherently wrong with that – but it wears thin. You can usually sense the difference between someone who documents their life and someone who curates a brand. One seeks connection; the other, attention.

I remember watching it unfold at Bonneville, the great salt flats where people chase land speed records. You'd see riders being shuffled around for sponsor photos, changing shirts between takes to satisfy different contracts, performing as much off the track as on it. They were busy – impressively so – but it all felt slightly removed from the essence of the thing. Then there were others: older riders, quiet teams, people sleeping in vans and tinkering under tarpaulins. They'd driven thousands of miles not to be seen, but to see what they were capable of. One man in his sixties, Canadian, I think, worked all night rebuilding his bike after it failed inspection. The next morning, he rolled onto the salt, ran 136 mph, nodded, and went back to his tools. No fuss. No post. No audience required.

That's what the Stoics mean when they say: Prioritise action. Don't talk about what you're going to do. Just do it. Don't share the plan – share the result. Or don't. Let your work speak. Let your integrity whisper.

Take Ken Miles – the brilliant but often overlooked British racing driver and engineer behind the development of the Ford GT40. He wasn't driven by ego, but by excellence. While others chased headlines and podium glitz, Miles was in the workshop, obsessing over gear ratios and handling dynamics. His fingerprints were all over the GT40's evolution, especially its endurance tuning for Le Mans. For Miles, it was never about the glory. It was about building something that could win – and knowing, deep down, that it was done right.

Even when corporate decisions robbed him of the triple-crown finish he rightfully earned in 1966, Miles didn't throw a tantrum or storm off in protest. He got back to work. His story reminds us that true mastery hides behind humility. Ego grabs the mic, but dedication builds legends.

Bonneville, of course, attracted people from both camps. Some were all about the image – there for the brands, the optics, the show. Others were chasing something quieter: a thrill, a goal they'd worked toward all their lives.

Being tied to a sponsor seemed to me just shy of madness. In the first few days at Bonneville, while waiting for the weather to clear, I watched people being herded around for photo ops. They spent more time on their phones than on the track – changing outfits, repeating interviews, making sure no sponsor name crossed into the wrong video take. It meant everything to them. And yet, it missed the point.

Bonneville is about the race. The dream. The long odds and the quiet triumph.

When I raced, I had one goal: to finish upright. The only deal I had to keep was with my little Lou inside. I had to be brave for her. And I was.

The photos and images I share now? They're not about sponsors, or brands – or even me. They're about you. My name doesn't matter. What I do doesn't matter. What matters is showing what's possible when you apply a Stoic mindset and shove those limiting self-beliefs where the sun doesn't shine.

As another martial arts giant and Stoic thinker, Glenn Morris, might have said: Study on this.

Every life – like every ride – offers a lesson. If you pay attention, you'll see the theme. One day it's patience. Another, courage. Sometimes it's the quiet discipline of simply showing up. Other times, the art of stepping aside. But every experience, every interaction, has something to teach. And ego is often the thing that blocks the learning. It says, "You already know."

"You're already good enough." "This isn't your fault." And just like that, you miss the off-ramp to growth.

The work is to stay open. Let others be bright. Let them have the spotlight, the applause, the front row. Let them lead the meeting, win the award, be the loudest in the room. If it matters to them, let it. You've got nothing to prove. You're not here to compete. You're here to become.

And becoming requires attention, humility, and action. Not noise. Not applause. Just the steady commitment to the path – whatever it asks of you next.

The Quiet Road

Humility is not self-erasure. It's not hiding. It's knowing that your worth doesn't depend on being seen. It's walking into a room without the need to take anything from it. No credentials required. No titles shouted across the table. The Stoics would call this *apatheia* – not apathy, but freedom from disturbance. Not needing to be more than you are, not less either. Just you, present and steady. Epictetus once said, "It is not he who reviles or strikes you who insults you, but your opinion that these things are insulting."[87] In other words, ego makes everything personal. Wisdom shrugs and carries on.

The most skilled people I've known rarely advertise it. The most impressive don't need you to know they're impressive. They just do the work. And they help others along the way, quietly, without a scorecard. They're the kind of people who fix the problem before you've noticed it's broken. The kind of people who stay up all night getting a stranger's bike past tech inspection. And when you thank them, they wave it off with a smile and change the subject. You learn more from those people than from a hundred self-appointed experts. And they remind you – gently, by example – that it's possible to live without performing.

As the popular saying goes, "People will forget what you said, but people will never forget how you made them feel." That doesn't come from ego. That comes from presence. From showing up as a whole human being and letting others be whole, too.

And if you still need a litmus test – if you still wonder whether you're acting from ego or from virtue – ask yourself, would I still do this if no one saw it?

Would you still write the song, cook the meal, make the gesture, take the ride, if there were no audience?

That's when you know it's real.

Ego is loud. Wisdom is quiet. One wants the loudest exhaust. The other, the smoothest line. And the ride – your life – gets smoother the moment you stop trying to prove something.

A few months before the world was thrown into a tailspin by the pandemic, and just a month or two after returning from Bonneville – still flushed with the high of it all – I met up with Ray for a bimble through the Sussex countryside. I was a different rider by then, shaped by the salt, the speed, the whole surreal experience. But not every change was for the better.

I was reckless. Not because the roads demanded it – but because my ego did. I'd just raced across the salt flats and was high on the thrill of it all. I wanted to show him how far I'd come from the woman who used to freeze at 50 mph. Look at me now.

We pulled into a café, and over a bacon sandwich, Ray said something I'll never forget. Gently, without judgement, just: "You don't need to do that."

That was it. No lecture. No drama. Just a quiet truth from a friend that hit exactly where it needed to. Because he was right – I did need to hear it.

We all have that voice in the helmet, that whisper that says, "Prove yourself. Go bigger. Be more." And we'll never get rid of it entirely. Like a coin needs both sides, ego will always ride with us. But it needs checking.

Ryan Holiday put it beautifully, quoting his friend Daniele Bollelli:

"Training is like sweeping the floor. Just because we've done it once, doesn't mean the floor is clean forever. Every day the dust comes back. Every day we must sweep."

So we sweep. And sweep again.

Not because we're flawed. But because we're still becoming.

So let others be bright. You don't need to outshine them to see your own path clearly. You don't have to fight to prove your worth, or shout to be heard. You're not here to compete. You're here to become.

Or as Chuck Norris once said – and yes, this is real – "Men are like steel. When they lose their temper, they lose their worth."

Stay sharp.

Chapter 11

Answer the Call

"At dawn, when you have trouble getting out of bed, tell yourself: I have to go to work — as a human being."
— Marcus Aurelius

IT'S MORNING AGAIN. THE kettle clicks but doesn't quite boil. The heating hasn't kicked in. Your phone glows with someone else's idea of urgency, and outside it's the sort of grey that doesn't even bother with rain – it just hangs there like a shrug. You lie there, not because you're tired exactly, but because you can't quite remember what's pulling you out of bed. Not today.

Marcus Aurelius knew this feeling. He called it what it was: resistance. Not laziness, not failure – just that very human moment when life asks something of you and your body hesitates. In his *Meditations* 5.1, he wrote, "At dawn, when you have trouble getting out of bed, tell yourself: I have to go to work – as a human being." That's the job. Just doing the work of being human.

It's easy to imagine the Stoics as stone-faced statues, untouched by doubt. But they wrestled too. Not with alarm clocks, admittedly, but with meaning. With how to act in a world that doesn't always offer applause. They didn't talk about purpose in the way modern job ads do – "must be passionate, driven, able to speak fluent Excel." No. For them, purpose wasn't something you found. It was something you lived. A kind of inner alignment between who you are and what you offer. They called this *oikeiôsis* – a word too long for breakfast but just right for the soul. It means fitting in with nature's pattern. Not in a passive way, like driftwood, but as an active participant in the human drama. You have an obligation – to treat others with respect and consideration, yes – but more than that: to recognise that we all belong to the same human family. That we're part of a greater whole. The Stoics believed this wasn't just idealism, it was reality. A role. A task. A reason.

Let's be honest: Not every day feels like a calling. Some mornings, you're not chasing purpose. You're chasing socks. But here's the question that lingers once the coffee is poured: *What makes an adventure matter?* It's not the distance. Not the scenery. Not the gear. What makes a ride – or a life – truly worthwhile is the reason behind it. The why that moves your feet to the floor before your brain has time to protest.

And that path doesn't need to be grand. We aren't all meant to be revolutionaries. Most of us won't cure diseases or write symphonies or make front-page news. But purpose doesn't care about scale. It cares about sincerity. Maybe your purpose is to raise kind children. Or to write something that helps just one person feel less alone. Or to be the sort of friend who shows up when things fall apart. That counts. That matters.

You don't need a grand destiny. Just something worth waking up for.

There's a kind of quiet courage in answering the call of an ordinary life with uncommon attention. Especially in a culture that tells you to chase happiness like it's on sale for a limited time only. The Stoics weren't interested in happiness. They were after fulfilment. Integrity. Purpose that didn't depend on outcome. Doing the right thing not because it guaranteed a result, but because it aligned with who they were.

And if all this sounds a bit abstract, let's return to something simpler: your feet on the cold floor. That first step. That first cup of tea. That's where purpose begins. Not in a TED Talk. Not in a midlife crisis. Just in the gentle insistence that you were made to participate. Not to drift. Not to perform. But to contribute. However quietly. However imperfectly.

So: What's calling you today?

Is it a road? A relationship? A conversation long overdue? Whatever it is, hear it. Honour it. And don't wait for it to feel heroic. Purpose often arrives dressed in very plain clothes.

The Engine That Starts Without Pushing

Some days, the engine refuses. You know the ones. You turn the key. There's a click, maybe a cough, and then – nothing. You curse, tap the tank and – depending on your bike – either pull the choke or fiddle with the key fob battery. Then, you try again.

Still nothing. You're suddenly bargaining with fate, as though your entire existence now hinges on whether the starter motor remembers its job. Riding, in these moments, feels like obligation. Like effort without joy. You question whether the route is worth it. Whether *you're* worth it.

But then there are other mornings. Mornings when the engine fires first time, clean and eager. No drama. No doubt. Just a low, satisfying hum that says, "Let's go." And you do. You're not dragging yourself to the road; the road seems to reach out and pull you forward. That's what purpose feels like. Not ease, exactly. But alignment. No pushing required.

The Stoics didn't ride motorcycles, of course. But they understood this principle better than most. For them, the human being – *you* – was designed for a function, a role within a larger order. Not fate, like some predestined career title carved into cosmic granite, but *purpose* – your unique contribution to a shared world. As Marcus Aurelius teaches, everything in nature plays its part, from horse to vine to human. The question is: What role will you fulfil? Not to impress, not to accumulate – but to serve something meaningful.

That doesn't mean your purpose needs to be heroic. It could be writing a book no one asked for, starting a community garden, or being the only one who smiles at the grumpy man behind the post office counter. Purpose is not about grandeur. It's about gravity – the quiet pull that makes even tired legs climb hills willingly.

Self-Determination Theory, a well-researched model in psychology, suggests we're most motivated when three needs are met: autonomy, competence, and relatedness.[88] In plain English: You want to feel free, good at something, and part of something bigger. Purpose checks all three boxes. It says, "You chose this. You've grown into it. And it matters." When those conditions align, motivation stops feeling like force. It feels like flow.

Even research into ageing shows that people with a strong sense of purpose live longer, handle stress better, and report deeper satisfaction.[89] Apparently knowing *why* you get out of bed makes a difference to how long you stay upright.

But the clearest proof, really, is your own experience. Think of a time when you were truly lit up by something. Not entertained. Not distracted. But engaged. Energised. The task might have been exhausting, but you ended the day with that rare kind of tired that feels . . . alive. That's purpose. That's what it means to ride not *to* something, but *from* something – an inner conviction, a pull that makes the uphill less brutal, and the destination less important than the going itself.

A Story from the Saddle: Writing This Book

For a time, I rode for the feeling. The hum of the engine, the wind curling through my jacket, the freedom of leaving without needing to explain where or why. There's a deep, clean pleasure in it – one you don't have to justify. But over time, I started noticing a strange feeling. As if the ride, however beautiful, was missing its weight. Something felt . . . unfinished.

I chalked it up to restlessness. Maybe I just needed more miles. A new landscape. Different weather. But no matter where I rode the feeling lingered. The trip always ended. The photo was taken. The story stayed in my head. The moments collected like dust on a shelf. They had no thread running through them.

The shift came when I began guiding. Not in the metaphorical sense, but literally – working as a tour guide. Which is funny, really, because I've always been a bit of a quiet one. Underneath the helmet, I'm not the charismatic alpha biker type. More Spock than Steve McQueen. I mean, I literally named my dog Spock. That should've been a clue.

But guiding changed something. Not the riding itself – that stayed magic. What shifted was everything around it. The stops, the side conversations, the long dinners under stars with people you'd only met three days earlier, yet suddenly knew by heart. I began to see that the riding was only half the joy. The other half was people. Their stories. Their questions. Their weariness and wonder. The laughter that came from real places, not polite ones.

You don't get that kind of connection in passing. Not in the work canteen. Not in the lift. Not with most neighbours. And honestly, how many of us actually know our neighbours? Know their dreams, their fears, their childhood regrets, their quiet hopes for a different life? I don't mean Christmas card-level acquaintance. I mean *knowing*.

That's what kept pulling me back. Because something inside me started to settle. Not loudly. Just a quiet shift. I realised that the rides didn't need more scenery. They needed meaning.

That's when I began writing. At first, it was just a project. A clever idea. A magazine article here or there, a blog post. Something to tinker with between trips, like fiddling with a carburettor for the sheer hell of it. But somewhere along the way, the engine turned over. I stopped needing to push. It became the thing that got me out of bed. No grand sense of destiny. Just quiet clarity.

I once heard it said that introverts spend energy in social situations, while extroverts gain it. That's true for me. I thrive in small groups, where the mask can slip. Where silence has room to breathe. Afterwards, I need time to reflect – to file the moments, turn them over, make sense of them. That part? That's glorious.

Seeing people not just as moving shapes on two wheels, but as whole, complex humans – it takes effort. It takes presence. But it's worth every drop.

This book became a turning point. No longer just a side project. It's a mission now. A way to share something that might – truly – help. Not in the "change your life in ten steps" way. But in the way that helps you notice you're already halfway there. That life is happening, whether you're on board or not. That time isn't waiting.

That's the message I always hoped to share on those rides across Europe or Africa. But most of the riders were already sold. They'd said yes to life. This book, though – it could land in the hands of someone still unsure. Someone waiting for a sign.

If that's you – don't wait. Don't dither. Every day is one day less.

Even if your adventure isn't a continent to cross, but a bridge to mend – that's purpose. That's meaning. That's growth. And it's worth it.

These days, I'm working more hours than ever. And I've never done that before. I have an energy I didn't know I had. A clarity I didn't expect. Because something clicked.

The fuel was always there.

I just hadn't found the right match.

Echoes and Ripples Through Time

Do you remember the last time time disappeared? Really disappeared – not scrolled away, not numbed out, but dissolved. Like it used to when you were nine, face lit by a torch under the covers, turning the pages of something far too advanced for your reading age. Or when the garden became a galaxy and your bicycle, a starship. That's the thing about purpose – it doesn't shout. It echoes. Faintly, but consistently. And the trick is not finding it, but listening closely when it returns.

For me, the breadcrumbs were always there: astronomy, sci-fi, nature documentaries with melancholy voiceovers, a glass of milk and a biscuit in bed. Airfix models, half-painted. Monty Python sketches that taught me it was OK to be weird – as long as you were funny. And always, the bicycle. I kept circling back to these things like a moth to a porch light, not knowing they were clues. Your childhood wasn't just play. It was pattern recognition. It was your body saying "ahhh yes" long before you knew the questions worth asking.

This book – or whatever this thing is – started as an idea. Something clever to do with all those motorbike stories and Stoic quotes I'd scribbled in notebooks over the years. But it didn't stay that way. Because every time I came back to it, I felt lighter. More awake. More like me. That, I've learned, is what purpose feels like. Not urgent. Just inevitable.

Stanislavski, the Russian theatre director who gave birth to method acting, wrote *An Actor Prepares* – a book that's technically about drama but is really about becoming. His whole premise was that you don't "play" a role. You *live* into it. As he put it, an actor should "experience" the part, not merely represent it. He even writes: "When an actor is completely absorbed by some profoundly moving objective so that he throws his whole being passionately into its execution, he reaches a state we call inspiration."[90]

I've borrowed that. When I cross the street or hesitate on a decision, I ask not, "What should I do?" but "Who do I want to be?" And then I act like that person. Even if it feels like a stretch. Especially when it does. My version is less poetic, but functional: *If you act like the person you want to be instead of the person you are, soon you'll be the person you want to be instead of the person you are.* Awkward? Slightly. But it works.

So: Who would you be proud to become?

Not famous. Not flawless. Just proud.

Because Stoicism, at its core, is not about what you think. It's about how you live. It's about whether your inner life matches your outer one. Marcus Aurelius didn't write *Meditations* to show off. He wrote it to survive himself. To leave behind something clear-eyed and useful – a ripple. You've felt that ripple, haven't you? From a teacher. A friend. A parent. A stranger who smiled at you when you were having a terrible day.

That's the thing: We're all making ripples. Every act of kindness is a kind of currency – one with infinite supply. Use it lavishly. Spend it often. Because somewhere out there, someone is waiting. For your voice. Your courage. Your story.

They don't need you to be perfect.

They need you to be real. In motion. Becoming.

Because someone out there needs your story to light the path of their own.

Reflection: Purpose Isn't Performance – It's Participation

Let's put something to rest. You don't need to have it all figured out. No one does. Not even the people who sound like they do – especially not them. Life isn't a puzzle you crack. It's a conversation. It whispers, it hints, it taps you on the shoulder during the washing up or just as your head hits the pillow. And your only job, really, is to turn toward it.

The Stoics didn't waste much time on elaborate theories. Epictetus didn't sit around pondering the meaning of life like a bearded contestant on *University Challenge*. He was too busy living it. He taught that philosophy is not something to admire on a shelf – it's something you carry in your pocket. You reach for it in traffic. You apply it when your patience thins. You use it when your kid asks why the world is unfair, and you realise you don't have a clean answer.

Purpose isn't about spectacle. It's not the job title, the follower count, or the dream you're supposed to be chasing because it looks good on paper. It's in the unnoticed moments. The times you smiled at the cashier not because you had to, but because you meant it. The colleague you mentored without a LinkedIn post to mark the occasion. The child you raised with patience on a day when your tank was bone dry. That's where meaning lives. In the small, quiet ripples.

And those ripples travel.

Seneca wrote, "Nature bids me do good to all mankind . . . Wherever there is a human being, there is the opportunity for kindness."[91] He never met a customer service chatbot, but the principle holds. Every act of love or courage gives someone else permission. It's contagious. Like yawning, but useful. When you stand up for what matters, you create space for others to do the same. You won't always see the effects. Most ripples never report back. But they go on – through time, through people, through generations. That's a kind of immortality. No temple required.

And before you ask – no, you don't need to be certain. You just need to be willing. Willing to risk looking foolish. Willing to begin. Willing to try, and fail, and try again in a slightly better-fitting jacket. The idea that you have to be "ready" is a stall. A very clever, socially sanctioned form of procrastination. Purpose doesn't arrive when you've done all the research. It arrives in motion.

Tuck this into your helmet, or your sock drawer, or the space just above your heart:

You were made for more than comfort – you were made for meaning.

Purpose is felt, not forced. Your calling may not be loud – but it's persistent. You don't need to be ready. You need to be willing. Your story matters – share it.

The world doesn't need more polish. It needs more participation. Your participation. Not the curated version, but the messy, honest, human one. You don't need to ride across continents or write a manifesto. You just need to keep showing up. With love. With effort. With heart.

You are not here to coast. You are here to contribute. Your ride is your message.

And finally – as the philosopher Chuck Norris never said (but probably meant to): *When purpose calls, don't send it to voicemail.*

Chapter 12

The Road Is the Teacher

"You, me, or nobody is going to hit as hard as life. But it ain't about how hard you're hit, it's about how hard you can get hit and keep moving forward."
— Rocky Balboa

LET'S START THERE — with a boxing quote, not a Roman philosopher. Odd? Maybe. But Rocky understood something Epictetus would've nodded at: The road doesn't reward appearances — it rewards endurance. Not just physical stamina, but emotional resilience. The capacity to keep going, eyes open, heart steady, even when the punches keep coming.

There's a myth — quiet but persistent — that life will eventually settle down. That the chaos will lift. That you'll hit some smooth stretch of tarmac and coast in comfort until the end. It's tidy. It's appealing. And it's nonsense. If you're lucky, life won't stop happening to you.

Adversity hurts. It doesn't always build character immediately. Sometimes it just builds resentment, confusion, or a strong urge to crawl under a duvet and stay there. But as Theodore Roosevelt pointed out, it's the very difficulty of the path that gives it value: "Nothing in the world is worth having or worth doing unless it means effort, pain, difficulty . . . I have never in my life envied a human being who led an easy life."[92] That doesn't mean you chase hardship like a masochist in search of virtue. But when the storm hits, it helps to remember: This is the curriculum. The obstacles are the syllabus. The road is the teacher.

Epictetus didn't mince words. In *Discourses* 1.24, life, as he put it, is like wrestling – not against some clumsy opponent, but against a strong, disciplined one who'll give you a proper thrashing, and in doing so, turn you into "Olympic-class material". That's quite a standard. You're not just trying to get through the day; you're preparing for the Games. Grief, disappointment, the creeping dread of irrelevance – each one is a sparring match. And in Stoic thought, the goal isn't to win. It's to wrestle well. To show up. To engage fully. To learn what you're made of, and maybe, become more than you were before.

The ancient Stoics weren't much concerned with happiness as we understand it – fleeting pleasure, external wins, bucket lists. They spoke instead of *eudaimonia* – not "happiness," but flourishing through virtue. You flourish not when life bends to your will, but when you live in alignment with your values. When you act with courage, justice, temperance, and wisdom. That's the gold standard. Not applause, not comfort, not likes. Just virtuous action, repeated in the hard moments.

Robert, from *Zen and the Art of Motorcycle Maintenance*, would've understood. He searched endlessly for "quality" – that elusive intersection of truth, beauty, and function. Something similar animates the Stoic: not perfection, but integrity. You ride the road not for scenery, but for the refinement it demands of you.

Thoreau didn't retreat to Walden Pond out of misanthropy – although it's possible he wasn't a fan of crowds – but because he wanted to live deliberately. To pay attention. To stop coasting. As he put it: "I went to the woods because I wished to live deliberately . . . and not, when I came to die, discover that I had not lived."[93] That line still lands. It's one thing to survive. Quite another to live. And living, in this deeper sense, means showing up to the road as it is – not the one you fantasised about, not the one you think you deserve. The one in front of you. Gravel, potholes, unexpected turns, and all.

We like stories with clean arcs. Start here. Learn something. Face adversity. Overcome. Grow. Cue sunset. Fade to credits. But life's a bit more Bukowski than that. Messier. Smudged. Bits fall off. People you love die. You make decisions you regret. You try to do the right thing and still somehow make a hash of it. No music swells in the background to reward your progress. And yet . . . the road teaches anyway.

Bukowski wrote, "What matters most is how well you walk through the fire."[94] Not how gracefully. Not how quickly. Just how well. There's something freeing in that. You don't need to glide. Just stay on your feet. You're still breathing. That means something's coming. It might be wonderful. It might be awful. Likely, a bit of both. You'll fall in love. You'll lose people. You'll start again. And again. The question is: How will you respond?

Every five to seven years, I've noticed something shifts. A quiet critical mass builds from everything you've absorbed – the joys, the losses, the lessons – and suddenly, you're no longer the same. You are not a fixed point. You are a process. You are not a noun, but a verb. A becoming. This is Stoic to the bone. The self is not something you protect. It's something you forge – through choices, through difficulty, through daily effort to close the gap between who you are and who you aspire to be.

There's power in how you narrate your life. The story you tell yourself – about your past, your pain, your mistakes – will shape your future more than any external event. As Brené Brown writes in *Rising Strong*, "When we deny our stories, they define us. When we own our stories, we get to write the ending."[95] You don't get to rewrite the facts, but you do get to reframe them. You choose the lens. And that lens can either trap you – or set you free.

It takes courage to face your circumstances and accept them – or even love them – for what they offer. But just as stones are smoothed by relentless waves, we too are shaped by life's seas. That's not sentimentality. That's philosophical clarity. Life isn't punishing you. It's sculpting you. Whether you flinch or face it is up to you.

Maybe you're at a crossroads. Or maybe one's coming. Don't flinch. Don't race toward false certainty. Don't cling to the old map just because it's familiar. Sit quietly. Check your compass. Ask yourself: What do I value? What would a virtuous response look like here?

Then act. Not with drama, not with bravado. Just with quiet conviction. Let the applause go. Let the noise fade. As Nelson Mandela wisely said, "May your choices reflect your hopes, not your fears." That's it. That's the road.

When I took to the road again, it wasn't for thrills or attention. It was a return to myself. A re-alignment.

I didn't become someone new – I remembered who I'd been all along.

When my ride is done, I want to skid sideways into the grave shouting: *Wow. What a ride!* And if I get just one more sentence after that, let it be this: "Thank you for my one wild and precious life."

That's not recklessness. That's presence. Gratitude sharpened by difficulty. And it's something you can cultivate – not by chasing novelty, but by paying close attention to your own experience.

The job is not to dominate the road. The job is to learn from it. It will teach you where your values lie. It will show you where you're fragile, and where you're strong. It will ask you to begin again, and again, and again.

Each mistake? A page in your handbook. Each grief? A chapter on loss. Each joy? A reminder of why we try. So, take the ride. Feel every bump. Sweat through the climbs. Laugh when you can. Cry when you must. But keep going.

Not because you're trying to win. But because you're trying to live – deliberately, courageously, with enough clarity to know what matters, and enough humility to let the rest go.

The answer lies on the road ahead. Time is precious. Don't waste the ride.

Epilogue

The Ride Continues

I DIDN'T WRITE THIS BOOK to teach you anything. I wrote it to remember what matters – and to share what I've learned from windswept roads, near-misses, and moments that cracked me open. I've learned what it means to go fast – not just in speed, but in trust. When you ride at 200mph, there's no room for doubt, no time to pretend. You have to be fully present. Fully honest. The lessons I found in that stillness-at-speed have followed me through every part of my life.

To ride is to pay attention. To respond, not just react. To manage risk with a calm hand. To feel fear and move anyway. These lessons aren't confined to the road. They're the same ones that shape a life.

If there's one truth the road keeps whispering, it's this: You don't have to be fearless. You just have to keep going. One step, one mile, at a time.

Whatever brought you here – a crossroads, a calling, or a quiet ache – I hope these pages reminded you that strength doesn't always roar. Sometimes it's the decision to try again. Sometimes it's asking for help. Sometimes it's choosing stillness when the world demands speed.

The truth is, I didn't get here on my own.

My invitation to the 200 mph club came not from privilege or pedigree, but from the kindness of strangers – people who believed in me before I did. My land speed records? Achieved on a secondhand bike I bought off eBay for less than the price of a new phone. None of it was planned. All of it was possible. And the courage I found? I saw it first in others.

Friends who taught me how to ride – and how to be resilient. Who showed me how to wring every last morsel of joy from the day, then go to bed, then get up and do it all again. On the road, I met people who revealed who they were without pretense. People who reminded me how wonderful humans can be – and how alike we really are, once you look just a little below the surface.

If I can offer one tip, it's this: Always try to go deeper. See things from others' perspectives. It will leave you richer, more compassionate, and more alive.

You can choose your life. Not the circumstances, maybe – but the meaning you bring to them. The line you take. The direction you grow.

In a world that rushes to judgement and clings to ego, love – not power – is the key to a peaceful heart.

And choice – quiet, stubborn, steady choice – is your greatest freedom.

So if you fall (and you will), don't panic.

Take a breath.

Pick your line.

And ride with virtue.

Where you look is where you go.

The Stoic Rider is the first in a series from Throttle & Thought Press. Future titles will explore deeper themes at the intersection of movement, meaning, and the mind.

Acknowledgments

No one rides alone. And this book is certainly proof of that.

To my family – thank you for always being in my corner. You've supported me in everything I've ever done, even when I vanished into my laptop or needed prompting to rejoin the rest of humanity.

Georgina and Jenna, you've been my greatest teachers and truest allies. You've helped me face big questions with clarity, reminded me what matters, and loved me even when I was off in another headspace.

Graham, thank you for always being there for me – just as big brothers are supposed to be. I still remember the early days when you took me with you to the pub, even though it probably wasn't the coolest thing to have your little sister tagging along. But you did it anyway. I always knew you were looking out for me – and you still are.

As a family, you've been my cheerleaders, my sounding boards, and the wisest friends I could have hoped for. When I reached crossroads, you helped me choose the line. When I doubted, you reminded me who I was.

To Robert – my writing partner. Thank you for helping me turn a noisy set of gears into a rideable rhythm. You reached the heart of me and helped me thread meaning through the stories.

To Alicia – designer, copy editor extraordinaire. Your thoughtful nudges peeled back layers I didn't realise I was still wearing. You invited more of me onto the page – and gave the book a face and form I could be proud of. You didn't just shape the visuals. You helped shape the voice.

To Lindsey – thank you for being a trusted guide, sounding board, and champion from the very beginning. You helped refine my public voice, steered me through the unknowns of publishing and marketing, and kept me moving forward when things felt overwhelming. I never felt alone with you riding beside me.

To Suzanne and Vito, who made sure I rode that white Hayabusa at Bonneville. As Suzanne puts it, they "got shit done." No fuss, no drama – just quiet loyalty and action.

To those who prefer to remain unnamed – thank you. You believed in me when the wheels were still wobbling. You rode beside me without judgment, handed me the flame when mine was fading, and reminded me – when it mattered most – why I had to rise. Because life doesn't always fight fair. And when it hits hard, you either stay down or get up swinging. I stood up because you showed me how.

To my mum and dad – sorry you weren't here to see this. I hope you would've been proud. I rode with you in my heart.

And to you, dear reader – thank you for being here. For picking up this book. For leaning into the wind with me. May it meet you where you are, and help you go wherever you need to.

Endnotes

1. Aurelius, *Meditations*, 6.8.
2. Epictetus, *Discourses*, 1.1.
3. Seneca, *Letters*, 91.
4. Aurelis, *Meditations*, 6.2.
5. Epictetus, *Discourses*, 1.1.
6. Frankl, *Man's Search for Meaning*, 77.
7. Aurelius, *Meditations*, 8.47.
8. Shakespeare, *Hamlet*, Act II, Scene II.
9. Chamberlain, *The Meaning of Prohairesis*, 149.
10. Rowling, text of speech.
11. Seneca, *Epistles*, 78.7.
12. Tedeschi & Calhoun, *Posttraumatic Growth*, 9.
13. Dweck, *Mindset*, 17.
14. Sartre, *Existentialism*, 17.
15. Seneca, *Moral Letters*, Epistle 71.
16. Aurelius, *Meditations*, 7.5)
17. Lawrence, *Seven Pillars*, 24.
18. Epictetus, *The Enchiridion*, 8.
19. Watts, *The Wisdom*, 37)

20. Nietzsche, *The Gay Science*, 276.
21. Aurelius, *Meditations*, 2.17.
22. Ibid, 8.33.
23. Epictetus, *The Enchiridion*, 8.
24. Ibid, 1.
25. Aurelius, *Meditations*, 7.56.
26. Ibid, 12.14.
27. Seneca, *Letters*, 2.
28. Pirsig, *Zen*, 277.
29. Seneca, *Moral Letters*, 101.
30. Jobs, "2005 Stanford Commencement Address."
31. Ware, "The Top Five Regrets."
32. Beck, *Finding Your Own*, 23.
33. Cleese and Booth, "Communication Problems."
34. Gershman and Daw, "Reinforcement."
35. Bartlett, *Remembering*, 197; Ghosh and Gilboa, "What Is A Memory," 104.
36. Greenberg, Solomon, and Pyszczynski, *The Worm*, 85.
37. Camus, *The Myth*, 3.
38. Frankl, *Man's Search for Meaning*, 82.
39. Ibid, 104.
40. Pyszczynski et al., "A Dual-Process Model," 835.
41. Epictetus, *Discourses*, 2.1.
42. Aurelius, *Meditations*, 4.47.
43. Seneca, *Moral Letters*, 13.
44. Vaughn et al., "Modulation."
45. Lindeblad et al., *I May Be Wrong*, 46.

46. Aurelius, *Meditations*, 8.48.
47. Csikszentmihalyi, *Flow*, 15.
48. Dscout, "Mobile Touches."
49. Seneca, *Selected Dialogues*, 161.
50. Aurelius, *Meditations*, 8.48.
51. Pirsig, *Zen*, 215.
52. Aurelius, *Meditations*, 7.9.
53. Thoreau, *Walden*, Chapter 1.
54. Waitzkin, "The Tim Ferris Show."
55. Hunter et al., "Urban Nature," 722.
56. Sturm et al., "Awe Walks," 1355.
57. Aurelius, *Meditations*, 104.
58. Pirsig, *Zen*, 4.
59. Seneca, *Letters*, 9.
60. Epictetus, *Discourses*, 1.4.
61. Pirsig, *Zen*, 4.
62. Bratman et al., "Nature."
63. Seneca, *On the Happy Life*, 135.
64. Beck, *Finding Your Own*, 32.
65. Epictetus, *Discourses*, 1.1
66. Yue and Cole, "Strength," 1114.
67. Maldonato, "The Ascending Reticular," 2.
68. Epictetus, *Discourses*, 2.5.
69. Aurelius, *Meditations*, 6.54.
70. Long, *Epictetus*, 8.
71. Eisenberger et al., "Does Rejection Hurt?", 290.
72. Carter, "Oxytocin Pathways," 17.
73. Durkheim, *The Elementary Forms*, 208.

74. Aurelius, *Meditations*, 2.1.
75. Lawrence, *The Mint*, 193.
76. Aurelius, *Meditations*, 2.1.
77. Manson. *The Subtle Art*, 160.
78. Casiday et al., "Volunteering," 6.
79. Okun et al., "Volunteering," 571.
80. Vaillant, *Triumphs*, 269.
81. Murray, *The Scottish*, 7.
82. Aurelius, *Meditations*, 10.16
83. Epictetus, *Discourses*, 4.
84. Plutarch, *Cato*, 5.
85. Long, *Hellenistic Philosophy*, 114.
86. Holiday, *Ego is the Enemy*, 62.
87. Epictetus, *Enchiridion*, §30.
88. Ryan and Deci, "Self-Determination," 68.
89. Hill and Turiano, "Purpose in Life," 1482.
90. Stanislavski, *An Actor Prepares*, 268.
91. Seneca, *De Vita Beata*, Chapter 24.2–3
92. Roosevelt, "Citizen in a Republic" speech.
93. Thoreau, *Walden*, Chapter 2.
94. Bukowski, *What Matters*, 9.
95. Brown, *Rising Strong*, 3

References

Books and Translations:

Aurelius, Marcus. *Meditations*. Translated by Gregory Hays. New York: Modern Library, 2006. Originally published ca. 180.

Bartlett, Frederic C. *Remembering: A Study in Experimental and Social Psychology*. Cambridge: Cambridge University Press, 1932.

Beck, Martha. *Finding Your Own North Star: Claiming the Life You Were Meant to Live*. New York: Harmony, 2002.

Brown, Brené. *Rising Strong: How the Ability to Reset Transforms the Way We Live, Love, Parent, and Lead*. New York: Random House, 2017.

Bukowski, Charles. *What Matters Most Is How Well You Walk Through the Fire*. Santa Rosa, CA: Black Sparrow Press, 1999.

Camus, Albert. *The Myth of Sisyphus and Other Essays*. Translated by Justin O'Brien. New York: Vintage Books, 1955.

Csikszentmihalyi, Mihaly. *Flow: The Psychology of Optimal Experience*. New York: Harper & Row, 1990.

Durkheim, Émile. *The Elementary Forms of Religious Life*. Translated by Karen E. Fields. New York: Free Press, 1995.

Dweck, Carol S. *Mindset: The New Psychology of Success*. New York: Random House, 2006.

Epictetus. *The Enchiridion*. Translated by Thomas W. Higginson. Mineola, NY: Dover Publications, 1995. Originally written ca. 125 CE.

———. *Discourses and Selected Writings*. Translated by Robert Dobbin. London: Penguin Books, 2002. Originally published ca. 108 CE.

Frankl, Viktor E. *Man's Search for Meaning*. Translated by Ilse Lasch. Boston: Beacon Press, 2006. Originally published 1946.

Holiday, Ryan. *Ego Is the Enemy*. New York: Portfolio, 2016.

———. *Stillness Is the Key*. New York: Portfolio, 2019.

Lawrence, T. E. *The Mint*. London: Jonathan Cape Ltd., 1955.

———. *Seven Pillars of Wisdom*. Edited by Angus Wilson. Hertfordshire: Wordsworth Editions, 2011. Originally published 1926.

Lee, Bruce. *Striking Thoughts: Bruce Lee's Wisdom for Daily Living*. Rutland, VT: Tuttle Publishing, 2000.

Lindeblad, Björn Natthiko, Navid Modiri, and Caroline Bankler. *I May Be Wrong: And Other Wisdoms from Life as a Forest Monk*. London: Bloomsbury, 2021.

Long, A. A. *Hellenistic Philosophy: Stoics, Epicureans, Sceptics*. 2nd ed. London: Bristol Classical Press, 1996. Originally published 1974.

———. *Epictetus: A Stoic and Socratic Guide to Life*. Oxford: Oxford University Press, 2002.

Manson, Mark. *The Subtle Art of Not Giving a F*ck: A Counterintuitive Approach to Living a Good Life*. New York: Harper, 2016.

Nietzsche, Friedrich. *Ecce Homo: How One Becomes What One Is*. Translated by Walter Kaufmann. New York: Vintage, 1967.

Nietzsche, Friedrich. *The Gay Science*. Translated by Walter Kaufmann. New York: Vintage Books, 1974. Originally published 1882.

Oliver, Mary. *New and Selected Poems, Volume One*. Boston: Beacon Press, 1992.

Pirsig, Robert M. *Zen and the Art of Motorcycle Maintenance: An Inquiry into Values*. New York: William Morrow, 1974.

Plato. *Five Dialogues*. Translated by G. M. A. Grube, revised by John M. Cooper. Indianapolis: Hackett Publishing, 2002. Originally published ca. 399 BCE.

Plutarch. *Cato the Younger*. Translated by John Dryden. Loeb Classical Library, 1919.

Seneca. *Letters from a Stoic*. Translated by Robin Campbell. London: Penguin Classics, 2004. Originally published ca. 65 CE.

———. *On the Shortness of Life: Life Is Long If You Know How to Use It*. Translated by C. D. N. Costa. London: Penguin Books, 2005. Originally published ca. 49 CE.

———. *Moral Letters to Lucilius*. Vol. 1. Translated by Richard Gummere. Loeb Classical Library, 1917.

———. *Selected Dialogues and Consolations*. Translated by Peter J. Anderson. Indianapolis: Hackett Publishing, 2015.

———. *On the Happy Life: De Vita Beata*. Translated by Andrew Stewart. Scotts Valley, CA: CreateSpace Independent Publishing Platform, 2016.

Stanislavski, Konstantin. *An Actor Prepares*. Translated by Elizabeth Reynolds Hapgood. London: Berg Publishers, 2013. Originally published 1936.

Thoreau, Henry David. *Walden; or, Life in the Woods*. Boston: Ticknor and Fields, 1854.

Vaillant, George E. *Triumphs of Experience: The Men of the Harvard Grant Study*. Cambridge, MA: Belknap Press of Harvard University Press, 2015.

Vickers, Joan N. *Perception, Cognition, and Decision Training: The Quiet Eye in Action*. Champaign, IL: Human Kinetics, 2007.

Watts, Alan. *The Wisdom of Insecurity: A Message for an Age of Anxiety*. New York: Pantheon Books, 1957.

Journal Articles:

Bar-Haim, Yair, et al. "Threat-Related Attentional Bias in Anxious and Nonanxious Individuals: A Meta-Analytic Study." *Psychological Bulletin* 133, no. 1 (2007): 1–24.

Bratman, Gregory N., Colin B. Anderson, Marc G. Berman, Brenna Cochran, Sjerp de Vries, Jack Flanders, et al. "Nature and Mental Health: An Ecosystem Service Perspective." *Science Advances* 5, no. 7 (2019): eaax0903. https://doi.org/10.1126/sciadv.aax0903.

Carter, Sue (formerly C. S.). "Oxytocin Pathways and the Evolution of Human Behavior." *Annual Review of Psychology* 65 (2014): 17–39.

Charles, Chamberlain. "The Meaning of Prohairesis in Aristotle's Ethics." *Transactions of the American Philological Association (1974–2014)* 114 (1984): 147–157. https://doi.org/10.2307/284144. Sartre, Jean-Paul. *Existentialism Is a Humanism*. Translated by Carol Macomber. New Haven: Yale University Press, 2007. Originally published 1946.

Eisenberger, Naomi I., Matthew D. Lieberman, and Kipling D. Williams. "Does Rejection Hurt?" *Science* 302, no. 5643 (2003): 290–92.

Gershman, Samuel J., and Nathaniel D. Daw. "Reinforcement Learning and Episodic Memory in Humans and Animals: An Integrative Framework." *Annual Review of Psychology* (2017).

Ghosh, Vedanta E., and Asaf Gilboa. "What Is a Memory Schema? A Historical Perspective on Current Neuroscience Literature." *Neuropsychologia* (2014).

Hill, Patrick L., and Nicholas A. Turiano. "Purpose in Life as a Predictor of Mortality Across Adulthood." *Psychological Science* 25, no. 7 (2014): 1482–86. https://doi.org/10.1177/0956797614531799.

Hunter, Mary R., Benjamin W. Gillespie, and Sophie Y. Chen. "Urban Nature Experiences Reduce Stress in the Context of Daily Life Based on Salivary Biomarkers." *Frontiers in Psychology* 10 (2019): 722.

Maldonato, N. M. "The Ascending Reticular Activating System: The Common Root of Consciousness and Attention." In *Smart Innovation, Systems and Technologies*, 26 (2014): 333–44. https://doi.org/10.1007/978-3-319-04129-2_33.

Okun, Morris A., Edward W. Yeung, and Sarah Brown. "Volunteering and Mortality Risk: A Meta-Analysis." *Psychology and Aging* 28, no. 2 (2013): 564–77. https://doi.org/10.1037/a0031519.

Pyszczynski, Tom, Jeff Greenberg, and Sheldon Solomon. "A Dual-Process Model of Defence Against

Conscious and Unconscious Death-Related Thoughts." *Psychological Review* 106, no. 4 (1999): 835–45.

Raichle, Marcus E. "The Brain's Default Mode Network." *Annual Review of Neuroscience* 38 (2015): 433–47.

Ranganathan, V. K., et al. "From Mental Power to Muscle Power – Gaining Strength by Using the Mind." *Neuropsychologia* 42, no. 7 (2004): 944–56. https://doi.org/10.1016/j.neuropsychologia.2003.11.018.

Reiser, Mathias, Dieter Büsch, and Jörn Munzert. "Strength Gains by Motor Imagery with Different Ratios of Physical to Mental Practice." *Frontiers in Psychology* 2 (2011): Article 194. https://doi.org/10.3389/fpsyg.2011.00194.

Richard G. Tedeschi and Lawrence G. Calhoun. "Posttraumatic Growth: Conceptual Foundations and Empirical Evidence." *Psychological Inquiry* 15, no. 1 (2004): 1–18. https://doi.org/10.1207/s15327965pli1501_01.

Ryan, Richard M., and Edward L. Deci. "Self-Determination Theory and the Facilitation of Intrinsic Motivation, Social Development, and Well-Being." *American Psychologist* 55, no. 1 (2000): 68–78. https://doi.org/10.1037//0003-066x.55.1.68.

Sturm, Virginia E., et al. "Awe Walks Promote Emotional Well-Being in Older Adults." *Emotion* 21, no. 7 (2020): 1352–62.

Vaughn, Daniel A., et al. "Modulation of Attention and Stress with Arousal: The Mental and Physical Effects of Riding a Motorcycle." *Brain Research* 1752 (2021): 147203. https://doi.org/10.1016/j.brainres.2020.147203.

Zak, Paul J. "The Neurobiology of Trust." *Scientific American* 293, no. 6 (2005): 88–95.

Reports and Government Publications:

Casiday, Rachel, et al. *Volunteering and Health: What Impact Does It Really Have?* Report to Volunteering England, 2008. https://www.researchgate.net/publication/228628782.

Department for Transport. *Reported Road Casualties Great Britain, Annual Report: 2022.* 2023. https://www.gov.uk/government/statistics/reported-road-casualties-great-britain-annual-report-2022.

Dscout. *Mobile Touches: Dscout's Inaugural Study on Humans and Their Tech.* 2019.

Transport Research Laboratory. *Cohort II: A Study of Learner and New Drivers (Volume 1 – Main Report).* 2008. https://www.broughtonschoolofmotoring.com/wp-content/uploads/cohrtiimainreport.pdf.

Speeches, Interviews, Podcasts, and Media:

Cleese, John, and Connie Booth, writers. "Communication Problems." *Fawlty Towers*. Season 2, Episode 1. Directed by John Howard Davies. Aired February 19, 1979. BBC.

Jobs, Steve. "Steve Jobs' 2005 Stanford Commencement Address." YouTube. June 2005. https://www.youtube.com/watch?v=UF8uR6Z6KLc.

Kubrick, Stanley. "Stanley Kubrick Interview." *Playboy*. March 1968.

Mercer, Dan. "My Left Foot Director Backs Calls for Actors to Stop 'Cripping Up.'" *Sky News*, June 19, 2021. https://news.sky.com/story/my-left-foot-director-i-would-cast-disabled-actor-in-daniel-day-lewis-role-if-film-was-made-today-12336232.

Roosevelt, Theodore. "Citizenship in a Republic." Speech, Sorbonne, Paris, France, April 23, 1910.

Rowling, J. K. "Text of J.K. Rowling's Speech." *Harvard Gazette*. June 5, 2008. https://news.harvard.edu/gazette/story/2008/06/text-of-j-k-rowling-speech/.

Timoney, Brian. "Daniel Day Lewis – Mad Or Our Greatest Method Actor?" *Brian Timoney*, August 19, 2014. https://briantimoneyacting.co.uk/daniel-day-lewis-mad-or-our-greatest-method-actor/.

Waitzkin, Josh. "Josh Waitzkin Distilled." Interview by Tim Ferriss. *The Tim Ferriss Show*. Podcast audio,

June 19, 2018. https://tim.blog/2016/11/27/tools-of-titans-josh-waitzkin-distilled/.

Washington, George. "Washington's Farewell Address, 1796." Lillian Goldman Law Library. https://avalon.law.yale.edu/18th_century/washing.asp.

Web Sources and Blogs:

Ware, Bronnie. "The Top Five Regrets of the Dying – A Life Transformed by the Dearly Departing." *Bronnie Ware*. Last modified 2024. https://bronnieware.com/regrets-of-the-dying/.

About the Author

LOUISA SWADEN IS THE voice behind The Existential Biker – where philosophy meets throttle, and courage takes the long way round.

Having not touched a motorbike for nearly twenty-five years, she went on to become the fastest woman on sand at Pendine Beach in Wales, rode on the salt flats of Bonneville, served as an ambassador for the Women Riders World Relay, and even broke a national record in powerlifting, all accomplished in her sixth decade. And now – she holds this book in her hands.

When she's not writing, guiding motorcycle tours, or travelling solo in her camper van with her dog, Spock, Louisa explores what it means to live fully, ask better questions, and follow the road that calls – even when it scares you.

The
STOIC
RIDER

COMPANION JOURNAL
A Guided Ride Through the Road Within

This journal belongs to:
_____

My dream bike is a:
_____

My perfect trip:
_____

Keep Riding.
Keep Reflecting.

Your next road is an inner one.

Download your free *Stoic Rider Companion Journal*, a space to go deeper with every chapter – filled with writing prompts, reflections, and room to make it your own.

Scan the QR code below

Or visit: existentialbiker.com/journal

*"What we notice, we can change.
What we name, we can carry with care."*
— Louisa

www.ingramcontent.com/pod-product-compliance
Lightning Source LLC
Chambersburg PA
CBHW020340010526
44119CB00048B/538